HISTORIC WOMEN OF MICHIGAN

HISTORIC WOMEN OF MICHIGAN

A SESQUICENTENNIAL CELEBRATION

Edited by
Rosalie Riegle Troester

Michigan Women's Studies Association   Lansing, Michigan

Copyright © 1987 by
Michigan Women's Studies Association
All rights reserved
including the right of reproduction
in whole or in part of any form

Published by
The Michigan Women's Studies Association
213 W. Main St.
Lansing, Michigan 48933

ISBN 0-9619390-0-1
Library of Congress Catalog Card Number 87-72894
Designed by Carol Shuler
Copy editing by Elizabeth Jones Waidelich
Manufactured in the United States of America
By Braun-Brumfield, Ann Arbor, MI

To Gerald C. Beckwith
September 9, 1930 – July 19, 1987
Beloved friend and supporter of the
Michigan Women's Studies Association

CONTENTS

Foreward	*ix*
Preface and Acknowledgements	*xiii*
Notes on the Contributors	*xxi*
Magdelaine Laframboise: Fur Trader and Educator	1
Keith R. Widder	
Sojourner Truth: Crusader for Women's Rights	15
Beverly Fish	
Laura Smith Haviland: Emancipator	25
Emily Dietrich	
Lucinda Hinsdale Stone: Champion of Women's Education	41
Gail Griffin	
Marion Marsh Todd: Populist Writer and Activist	61
Pauline Adams and Emma S. Thornton	
Mary Mayo: Leader of Rural Women	73
Marilyn Culpepper	
Anna Howard Shaw: Orator	89
Dorothy and Lawrence Giel	
Ella Wing Merriman Sharp: Conservationist	103
Lynne Loftis and Natalie Field	
Caroline Bartlett Crane: Minister to Sick Cities	117
O'Ryan Rickard	
Bertha Van Hoosen: Surgeon	135
Clara Raven	
Voltairine de Cleyre: Social Visionary	143
Blaine McKinley	
Mary Chase Perry Stratton: Entrepreneurial Artist	155
Grace Stewart	
Martha Longstreet: Children's Doctor	171
Evelyn Shields	

Mary Carmelita Manning: Founder of Mercy College of Detroit	185
Susan Elizabeth Bakke	
Ana Clemenc: Heroine of the Copper Miners	197
Virginia Law Burns	
Marguerite Lofft de Angeli: Writer and Illustrator for Children	205
K. Fawn Knight	
Loleta Dawson Fyan: State Librarian	217
Emma S. Thornton	
Genevieve Gillette: Landscape Architect	233
Miriam Easton Rutz	
Harriette Simpson Arnow: Author	247
Sharon M. Rambo	

FOREWARD

As President of the Michigan Women's Studies Association, I am pleased to present to you this collection of essays on the lives of historic Michigan women. These papers were commissioned especially for this anthology and most of them were presented in draft form at the MWSA Annual Conference held in May of 1987.

The Michigan Women's Studies Association (MWSA) was founded in 1973 to provide support and encouragement for the women's studies courses and programs which at that time were just beginning to develop in the universities, colleges, and public schools of Michigan. The majority of the members of the Association were educators and to achieve its goal, the Association sponsored an annual conference and published a quarterly newsletter.

As time progressed, the membership of the Association grew, with more members coming from the community at large. We also became aware that women's studies courses and programs, although increasing in strength and number, usually reached only those enrolled on college campuses. Our organization wished to reach out to the community and to involve a larger number of learners in our educational programs. As an Association, too, we were becoming aware of the lack of information on the history of women generally and on the history of Michigan women particularly.

From these realizations came the concept of the Michigan Women's Historical Center and Hall of Fame. We envisioned an off-campus facility which would house exhibits giving recognition to the achievements of Michigan women and would enhance public awareness of the role Michigan women have played in the development of our state. Such a center would also be the basis for community outreach in support of women's studies programs as well as a clearinghouse for social and historical documents and related reference materials.

In 1980, the Association found what we believed to be the ideal setting for such a facility: the historic Cooley Haze House, located in downtown Lansing. We were successful in obtaining a $1.00 a year lease on this property and began fundraising efforts to restore the building to its former elegance. We also began the development of the selection process for those inducted into the Michigan Women's Hall of Fame. In 1983, we held the first "Celebration of Michigan Women" and inducted some seventeen women into the Michigan Women's Hall of Fame. Among the first honorees were Sojourner Truth, Laura Smith Haviland, Anna Howard Shaw, and Lucinda Hinsdale Stone. Since then we have held three additional inductions recognizing some forty-four contemporary and historic Michigan women. Three of the women whose lives are described in this anthology are represented on the medallion given to living members of the Hall of Fame.

After seven years of fundraising, the Center was dedicated and opened to the public on June 10, 1987, the year of the Michigan Sesquicentennial. It contains exhibits recognizing Hall of Fame Honorees, an Art Gallery which features changing shows by Michigan artists and photographers, and meeting rooms which are being used by a variety of women's groups from across the state. It is becoming the community outreach facility which we had envisioned some seven years earlier.

The women whose lives are explored in these essays are all either nominees or honorees in the Michigan Women's Hall of Fame. They have also been recognized in a Theme Trail Program. This program consists of commemorative signs which are placed at a variety of sites thoughout Michigan and described on an illustrated brochure. <u>Historic Women of</u>

<u>Michigan: A Sesquicentennial Celebration</u> is the first publishing venture of the MWSA. All of these efforts reflect the ongoing commitment of the Association to reach out to the people of our state.

Gladys Beckwith, President
Michigan Women's Studies Association

PREFACE AND ACKNOWLEDGEMENTS

The history of women, or "herstory" as some metaphorically call it, is a relatively new and tremendously exciting field. I, myself, am not a historian but a teacher of writing who became intrigued with the possibilities of women's untold stories through my involvement with the Michigan Women's Studies Association. What I had envisioned as routine academic service changed my life and radically altered my view of women and our place in the world. One of the results of this change is this anthology, a collection of historical essays on Michigan women. For some readers, these biographies will restate long-held notions of women's place in history. For others, the essays will prompt a re-vision of their thinking and perhaps spark a search for information on other foremothers. It is my hope that the book will serve as a bond to all readers, uniting us to these strong women from our past whose actions continue to shape our lives.

Women's history is revisionist by nature. It looks at what has been thought and taught in new ways and with different methods than traditional historians. Each of the authors represented within has used non-traditional research methods and looked with new lenses at traditional historical materials. A summary of these methods, as described by the essayists, appears below and may help readers to conduct their own research and write their own histories.

Reference librarians will be the researcher's best friends as they are professionally trained in accessing hard-to-find material. Important old books may sometimes be found in local libraries. They often keep material on people who originally held interest only to local historians. The collections of older universities can be good sources for material on their notable graduates. Smith College has begun an extensive women's history recovery project and Radcliffe College houses the Arthur and Elizabeth Schlesinger Library on the History of Women in America.

Archival material is also extremely valuable but sometimes hard to access or to work with once one finds it. Archives often contain interesting holographic letters and other documents and the excitement one feels when confronted with these primary sources makes it worthwhile to work at deciphering spidery handwriting. Subjects such as Caroline Bartlett Crane kept a rich storehouse of personal and public documents, but women less conscious of their contribution to the state, such as Ana Clemenc, kept no such records. The American Library Directory lists well-known archives. The National Union Catalog of Manuscript Collections can help to find obscure records, and so can resourcefulness, ingenuity, and persistance. The records of clubs and organizations often contain hitherto hidden information and can be especially revealing documents of social history.

Oral interviews provide much of the material in this volume, both those conducted by the writers themselves and those recorded by others and deposited in such libraries as the Bentley Historical Library at the University of Michigan. Respondants are often able to contribute family letters and other records in addition to answering questions and telling stories. Newspaper archives called "morgues" can provide valuable, if often unverifiable, material. One caveat about factual discrepancies: time often distorts and both published and oral histories frequently disagree on dates and other facts. References in older works are often obscure or less carefully documented; therefore, beginning researchers need to consult respected secondary sources in order to put their subjects in context and to compare their findings with those of others more experienced in the historical period under scrutiny.

Some of the subjects described in this anthology kept diaries or published an autobiography. Emily Dietrich relied heavily on the autobiography of her subject, Laura Smith Haviland, and had this to say about a feminist perspective on such use:

> I used her own view of her life in determining which events and activities were important. I listened to her voice and read her prose carefully as a way to understand her personality. I realized that an autobiography must, by nature, be biased, but the biases, once revealed, are interesting in themselves. Haviland's interests differ from a biographer's. She wrote to inspire action, not to produce a definitive text about her life. Yet the spirit behind the book makes it invaluable because it includes not only the facts but the force and character that made her life worth remembering.

Feminist scholarship as a whole has made a commitment to the personal voice as a means to truth; thus, no attempt has been made to force these essays to match each other in tone or style or to fit them into the mold of traditional scholarship. While some of the biographies have been deeply edited, I trust that each essay still shines with the relationship the author sustains with his or her subject. These relationships range from the collegiality between biographer Clara Raven and Bertha Van Hoosen to the academic admiration Bev Fish shows toward her subject, Sojourner Truth.

One of the problems faced by copy editor Elizabeth Waidelich and me was the use of surnames. For too long, writers have diminished women by calling them by their first names, even when adult. To eliminate this sexist practice, we have adopted the style traditionally used when writing about men and have used last names alone. Occasionally this results in an awkwardness, as when the subject is young and unmarried or when she marries late in life, as did Margaret Chase Stratton. In some of these cases, we have sacrificed editorial uniformity to felicity of style and used given names. Similarly, when both a woman and her husband are referred to in the same sentence, we resisted the temptation to simply reverse the practice of earlier historians, thus making it "John and Adams" where it was originally "Adams and Abigail." We opted for equality and called them both by their first names.

Although the women whose biographies appear herein are remarkable for their diversity, some comparisons and correspondences are possible. I mention only a few here and invite the reader to find more. Both Mother Carmelita Manning, founder of Mercy College, and author Harriette Simpson Arnow came to Detroit in the 1940s and were caught in the frantic economy of World War II. Lucinda Stone and Ella Sharp both realized the importance of the women's club movement in achieving goals for women. Medical doctors Bertha Van Hoosen and Martha Longstreet chose professions which accorded them public esteem within their lifetime, while others suffered neglect and sometimes ridicule for their work. Several used the written word to accomplish their goals, and Caroline Bartlett Crane and Anna Howard Shaw were accomplished orators. Shaw, like social visionary Voltarine DeCleyre, landscape architect Genevieve Gillette, and many of the others, never married, but some of the women juggled the demands of family and public service in the days when such a mix was exceptional.

Yet the subjects of these commissioned essays are diverse, as diverse as the experiences of the untold women who have contributed to the making of Michigan and the shaping of our nation. As Gail Griffin writes in the introduction to her essay on Lucinda Hinsdale Stone:

> the remarkable women whom we research and celebrate in this volume serve not only as singular inspirations, but also as lenses which allow us to see the more general experience of women at a given historical moment. We should regard these women bifocally, as figures simultaneously exceptional and representative, figures in whose lives we can trace another, larger life, that of Common Woman, who stands for all.

The Sesquicentennial of the state of Michigan provides a focus for the work of the Michigan Women's Studies Association in its continued recovery of lost histories of important women, including those who were active in the state, those who came to the state in later years, and those who went forth from Michigan to accomplish their goals throughout the world. This anthology has been partially supported by a sesquicentennial grant from the Michigan Council of the Humanities under the "Making of Michigan" program initiative. Under the terms of the grant, 500 public libraries within the state received complimentary copies of the book. The grant also enabled most of the authors represented herein to present drafts of their essays to the eleventh annual MWSA conference in May of 1987.

Credit goes to Patricia D'Itri, Professor of American Thought and Language at Michigan State University, for both project conception and grant writing. Thanks also to the grant-writing efforts of Dr. D'Itri, the Michigan Department of Commerce funded a companion grant as part of its Sesquicentennial YES 150 Project. Under this grant, the Michigan Women's Studies Association developed a theme trail recognizing distinguished Michigan women, including many of those anthologized here.

Editing this anthology has been generally a joy. It has truly been a collective endeavor: all the authors have been cooperative and prompt in returning manuscripts; the wonderful copy editor, Elizabeth Jones Waidelich, has read carefully over half the essays; and my fellow members of the Board of Directors of the Michigan Women's Studies Association have been most supportive, contributing time, energy, and ideas. President Gladys Beckwith, Treasurer Louise Shumway, the late Gerald C. Beckwith, Board member Antonio J.A. Pido, Beth Ellen Woodard, and Elizabeth Giese, Education Director of the Michigan Women's Historical Center, assisted in grant implementation.

I wish to thank Saginaw Valley State College for granting me a sabbatical, thus giving me the time necessary for the editing and publishing tasks. The college also provided the computer equipment, software, and secretarial services so that we could produce camera-ready copy. Gayle Leece stepped in at the last minute to contribute her time and talent in layout. She has my heartfelt thanks for designing the photography pages. Edward E. Lewis, President of Lewis Publishing Company of Chelsea, Michigan, has been my mentor and my guide throughout this book, the first publishing effort of the MWSA. Under his tutelage, I completed the equivalent of a graduate course in publishing, one taught by a capable, compassionate, and wise professor.

Without Carol Shuler, this book would not have been completed. Her knowledge of word processing and ability to organize are matched only by her prodigious typing speed and infinite patience. She contributed design ideas along with Ed Lewis and I see her as the most important member of the team which produced the book. Thank you, Carol, from the depths of my harried heart.

While all the essays were commissioned expressly for this volume, several have been published or will be published in different forms. The essay on Marion Todd appeared in a different form in "A Rehabilitation: The Writer and Populist Activist Marion Marsh Todd" by Pauline Adams and Emma S. Thornton in The Society for Study of Midwestern Literature Newsletter, Volume II, Number 1, Spring, 1981, pp. 1-13; material in "Ana Clemenc, Heroine of the Copper Miners" by Virginia Law Burns appears in more detail in her Tall Annie, a juvenile biography. "Bertha VanHoosen, Physician" appeared in The Journal of American Medical Women's Association of July, 1963, which grants copyright permission; Emma Thornton holds the copyright to "Loleta Fyan, State Librarian," printed herein with permission, and to Loleta and the Evergreen Tree, a full-length biography in progress.

No photograph of Magdelaine Laframboise is available. As a symbol of this métis fur trader, we chose a sketch by Patricia Boodell showing a beaded beaver pelt. (Sonia Bleeker, The Chippewa Indians (New York: Willian Morrow, 1955). The photograph of Mary Mayo is printed with permission of the Michigan State University Archives and Historical Collections; the photo of Loleta Fyan is copyright Backrach; and the photo of Marguerite DeAngeli is copyright Bart Costanzo. We thank all those mentioned for permission to reprint materials.

Rosalie Riegle Troester
September 15, 1987

NOTES ON THE CONTRIBUTORS

Pauline Adams is an Associate Professor of American Thought and Language at Michigan State University. She has co-authored a book with Emma Thornton and written more than 20 articles. Born and educated in the East, she calls herself a naturalized midwesterner. Her research interests range widely across the American scene.

Susan Elizabeth Bakke is a 1987 graduate of Mercy College of Detroit. She is currently employed as a representative with Maxicare insurance and plans to finish a Masters in English literature.

Gladys Beckwith has been president of the Michigan Women's Studies Association since 1973 and is the founding mother of the Michigan Women's Historical Center and Hall of Fame. She is Professor of American Thought and Language and former coordinator of the Women's Studies Program at Michigan State University from which she received her doctorate in English Education. She is a member of the Lansing Board of Education and has a research interest in Irish feminism.

Virginia Law Burns freelanced as a magazine and newspaper writer before turning to juvenile non-fiction. She has taught creative writing and edited a regional magazine and a newsletter. Her published biographies include <u>William Beaumont, Frontier Doctor</u>; <u>Lewis Cass, Frontier Soldier</u>; <u>First Frontiers</u>; and <u>Tall Annie</u>.

Marilyn Mayer Culpepper is a professor of American Thought and Language at Michigan State University. A frequent collaborator on papers and essays on 19th century women, she is co-author with Perry E. Gianakos of a composition text, Writing For Life.

Emily Ann Dietrich teaches English at Detroit Country Day School in Birmingham, Michigan. She shares her loyalty between two places celebrating their 150th birthdays this year: the state of Michigan and Mount Holyoke College, where she earned a B.A. She also has an M.A. from the University of Michigan.

Natalie Field received her B.A. from Smith College and is Docent and Historian at Ella Sharp Museum in Jackson, Michigan. Her research interests are women's history and Victorian life.

Beverly Fish is currently completing a Ph.D. in American History at Wayne State University. As a member of the Michigan Sesquicentennial Speaker's Bureau, she has presented her paper on the life of Sojourner Truth to audiences across the state of Michigan.

Dorothy Giel holds two masters from Central Michigan University, one in English education and one in speech. She is a real estate agent for Concept I in Big Rapids.

Lawrence Giel holds a masters from Winona State University and a doctorate from Ball State University. He teaches in the Social Science Department at Ferris State College.

Gail Griffin is Associate Professor of English and Coordinator of Women's Studies at Kalamazoo College. She received her doctorate from the University of Virginia. Publications include Emancipated Spirits: Portraits of Kalamazoo College Women.

Fawn Knight teaches English at Michigan Christian College in Rochester, Michigan. She received her Ph.D. in Reading and Children's Literature from Oakland University and has published articles in such journals as Top of the News and Children's Literature in Education.

Lynnea Loftis is Curator of Historical Education and Interpretation at Ella Sharp Museum in Jackson, Michigan. She graduated from Spring Arbor College and, shares with co-author Natalie Field an interest in women's history and Victorian life.

Blaine McKinley is Professor of American Thought and Language at Michigan State University. He is interested in the history of American anarchism and is currently working on an essay about anarchist-feminist novels. His earlier articles on American anarchists have appeared in American Quarterly, Journal of American Culture, and Labor History.

Sharon Rambo is a graduate of Carnegie-Mellon and Michigan State Universities. She is an assistant professor at Michigan State, where she teaches women's studies and writing.

Clara Raven, M.D. is a retired colonel in the United State army and Deputy Chief Medical Examiner of Wayne County, Emeritus. A pathologist and microbiologist who pioneered research in Sudden Infant Death Syndrome (SIDS), Dr. Raven was admitted to the Michigan Women's Hall of Fame in 1987.

In addition to numerous research studies, she has published "History of Women in the Medical Corps of the U.S. Army" and is co-author of a Japanese textbook on histopathology.

O'Ryan Rickard, a journalist, is general manager and advisor of the Western Herald at Western Michigan University and adjunct instructor in humanities at Nazareth College. He has graduate degrees in American history and English from Western Michigan University.

Miriam Easton Rutz received both her B.S. and M.S. in Landscape Architecture. She practiced in California and Arizona before beginning her teaching career at Michigan State University. Women's influence on the landscape is one of her focus areas. She chaired the American Society of Landscape Architect's Committee on Women in Landscape Architecture Education and was the first woman to be President of the Council of Educators in Landscape Architecture.

Evelyn Shields received her doctorate from the University of Michigan and teaches humanities and communications at Delta College. She is president of the Historical Society of Saginaw County and has edited two books, The Bicentennial History of Saginaw County and A Medical History of Saginaw County.

Grace Stewart is currently the Director of the Focus on Women Program at Henry Ford Community College. She received her Ph.D. in English from Wayne State University and is interested in feminists of all disciplines. She has published A New Mythos: The Novel of the Artist as Heroine.

Emma Shore Thornton is an assistant professor emeritus of Michigan State University. She is the author of <u>The Stone in My Pocket and Other Poems</u> and co-author with Pauline Adams of <u>A Populist Assault: Sarah E.V. Emery on American Democracy</u>. She is presently completing a full-length biography of Loleta Fyan, entitled <u>Loleta and the Evergreen Tree</u>.

Rosalie Riegle Troester is Associate Professor of English at Saginaw Valley State College and Vice President of the Michigan Women's Studies Association. She teaches writing and women's studies and is working on an oral history of the Catholic Worker movement.

Keith R. Widder has been Curator of History for the Mackinac Island State Park Commission since 1971. He has an M.A. in history from University of Wisconsin-Milwaukee. His current research interest is the métis population of Mackinac Island.

MAGDELAINE LAFRAMBOISE (1780 - 1846)

MAGDELAINE LAFRAMBOISE, FUR TRADER AND EDUCATOR

Keith R. Widder

During the early decades of the nineteenth century, métis women, as those of Indian-French descent are called, contributed much to the development of the fur-trade society which revolved around Mackinac Island, Michigan. Magdelaine Laframboise was one of these women. Laframboise was not only a successful businesswoman; she also devoted her financial resources and time to educating youth, providing for the poor, and furthering the practice of Roman Catholicism. Throughout her life, she never lost contact with either side of her dual heritage: Ottawa and French Canadian. After the War of 1812, the society in which she had lived all of her life changed significantly as American settlers and institutions came to stay at Mackinac, but Laframboise found acceptance among the newly arriving American businessmen, government agents, military men, and missionaries and helped to bring about the transformation of her society.[1]

Magdelaine was born in 1780 to Jean Baptiste Marcot and Marie Neskech. Marcot, a French-Canadian, engaged in the fur trade for many years in the western Great Lakes region, but he died shortly after his daughter's birth. She was raised by her mother, the daughter of the Ottawa Chief Kewinaquot (Returning Cloud), in the Ottawa village along the Grand River at Grand Haven. On August 1, 1786, Father Louis Payet baptized Magdelaine in Ste. Anne's Church on Mackinac Island. For the rest of her life, she faithfully observed the rites and practices of her father's religion.[2]

Sometime in 1794 or 1795 Magdelaine married the French-Canadian fur trader, Joseph Laframboise. It was a common practice for Catholic men who engaged in the fur trade to take Ottawa or Chippewa women as wives and later to formalize the relationship before a visiting priest at Mackinac. On July 11, 1804, Father Jean Dilhet solemnized their marriage after Joseph and Magdelaine exchanged vows before him in Ste. Anne's.[3] The couple's first child, Josette, was born on September 24, 1795; four years later Father Gabriel Richard baptized her at Mackinac before her Godparents, Josette Adhemar and Isidore Lacroix.[4] In 1806, a son, Joseph, was born to Magdelaine and Joseph.

Joseph traded for furs among the Ottawa living along the Grand River. Generally, he and Magdelaine followed the annual cycle of the fur trade. In summer, at Mackinac, they would exchange the previous winter's fur harvest for a fresh supply of trade goods. Included among these items were blankets, axes, brass kettles, knives, beads, and muskets to be traded for furs gathered by Ottawa hunters and trappers. In autumn, Joseph and Magdelaine would load their merchandise into a batteau and head down Lake Michigan to the mouth of the Grand River at Grand Haven. From there, they would proceed upstream to their winter post near Ada where they carried on their commerce.

In the fall of 1806, Joseph and Magdelaine, along with boatmen, young Joseph, and their Indian slave, Angelique, left Mackinac to carry on their usual commerce at their winter post. This time, however, disaster struck them. While camped on the beach only a day away from Grand Haven, Laframboise was saying his nightly prayers on his knees when a disgruntled Indian shot him dead. Apparently, earlier in the day

Laframboise had refused his assassin's request for liquor. Although widowhood descended upon Magdelaine quickly and without warning, she carried on with composure and resolution. She transported Joseph's body to Grand Haven for burial. From there she continued on to her winter camp and operated the family's business on her own.[5]

For the next two decades, LaFramboise lived through great changes occurring in the northwestern Great Lakes region. Although American soldiers had first occupied Fort Mackinac in 1796, the United States' hold on the area was tenuous. Furthermore, British and Canadian traders controlled the fur trade and reaped most of its profits. In 1812, a British and Indian force from St. Joseph's Island captured Mackinac Island. Three years later, the Treaty of Ghent returned Mackinac to the United States forever. Hereafter, the rapidly expanding American nation not only controlled Mackinac but extended its authority west to the Mississippi River and beyond. Farmers, entrepreneurs, ministers, teachers, government agents, and soldiers brought American political, economic, and social institutions to the fur-trade society. This intrusion presented members of this traditional society with a serious challenge to their way of life. Laframboise showed remarkable ability to accommodate herself to change, but she also continued to practice customs of her own French and Ottawa heritage.

At her husband's death, Laframboise assumed responsibilities for conducting the family's business and distinguished herself as a successful businesswoman. This was not an easy task. The fur trade was largely controlled by men, although other métis women also achieved considerable success in the trade. Among these women were Magdelaine Laframboise's sister, Therese Schindler, and Elizabeth Mitchell, the wife of the British physician and trader Dr. David Mitchell.[6] Laframboise's business accomplishments earned her respect from all members of the fur-trade society, including Indian agent Henry Schoolcraft, missionary William Ferry, and fur trade employee, Gurdon Saltonstall Hubbard.

Prior to the War of 1812, Laframboise ran her business in the same manner as had her husband, but after the war she accommodated herself to John Jacob Astor's American Fur Company. By 1816, Astor had forced his Canadian partners to sell their interests south of the Canadian border to him, and he moved to monopolize the trade.[7] Although he never completely eliminated all of his competitors, most traders either came to be employed by the American Fur Company or traded at their own risk with the understanding that they sell their furs to Astor. Laframboise appears to have worked in both capacities. Her name appears on an 1818 list of company employees with the designation that she had been "engaged at Mackinac" and "employed at Grand River."[8] During 1822, she traded at her own risk in conjunction with Rix Robinson, who then purchased her business. The year before, Laframboise worked "For Account and Risk of the American Fur Company."[9] Each year she had to submit to the regulations of the United States government when she procured a license to trade from the United States Indian agent residing on the Island.[10] Her ability to adapt to the presence and power of the giant American Fur Company enabled her to prosper financially in the midst of great change.[11]

Upon Laframboise's retirement, the Ottawa chiefs, recognizing their common blood relationship, presented to her one section of land along the Grand River near Ada. In addition, they gave another section to her son Joseph, and yet one more section jointly to her grandchildren, Benjamin Langdon Pierce (deceased) and Josette Harriet Pierce.[12] This show of affection indicated that the métis fur trader had maintained close and friendly ties with her mother's people throughout the years.

Magdelaine Laframboise

Magdelaine Laframboise faithfully provided for the needs of her children and kept constant vigilance for their well-being. Before her husband's death, she sent her daughter to Montreal for education, an experience she had been denied. Josette benefitted greatly from her stay in Montreal as she became acquainted with Euro-American ways. At Mackinac during the winter of 1815-16, she met and fell in love with Captain Benjamin K. Pierce of the Artillery, who had come to Fort Mackinac when the American army regarrisoned the post after the War of 1812. (Pierce's brother Franklin was elected President of the United States in 1852.) Josette and Benjamin were married in a civil service on April 2, 1816, while Josette's mother was away. Upon her return, an elaborate second wedding was held at Elizabeth Mitchell's large house on Market Street. Laframboise, dressed in her Ottawa clothing, welcomed the captain's fellow officers, their families, and two island families. Unfortunately, the newlyweds enjoyed only a short life together, for Josette and her son both died in 1821. Daughter Josette Harriet survived, and her grandmother made considerable effort to provide for her welfare.[13]

Laframboise took her son, Joseph, to Montreal by canoe so he could attend school. There she placed him under the direction of her nephew, Alexis Laframboise. Alexis put Joseph in a French school where he learned to read the catechism. On May 8, 1819, Alexis joyfully reported that Joseph would take his First Communion later in the month. This news must have warmed the heart of his devout mother back at Mackinac. Alexis touched upon the close bond between mother and son in referring to Joseph's upcoming communion: "Oh what a beautiful day for him. How much he must thank God to keep for him such a good mother who does everything in order to procure his happiness."[14] Magdelaine sent money to Alexis to defray Joseph's education costs. She received what she considered a good return on her investment as Joseph learned to read and write--skills which his mother did not learn until after her forty-first birthday.

Laframboise could speak fluent French, English, Ottawa and Chippewa, but as of August 21, 1821, she was unable to write her name in any language.[15] Some time later, however, she apparently learned to read and write both French and English. Perhaps she received instruction from the Reverend William M. Ferry and his associates after they opened a boarding school on the Island for Indian and métis children. In fact, Ferry, a Presbyterian minister, rented part of Laframboise's house in November, 1823, as the first site for his school and the home for twelve boarding students. Her kind feelings toward the Presbyterians greatly encouraged Ferry who believed that her influence among the Indians would help him to obtain students for his school.[16] No doubt, Laframboise had little interest in Ferry's Protestant Christianity, but she eagerly supported his educational efforts, thereby helping to facilitate the implantation of another American institution--evangelical Protestant religion.

Most likely Laframboise learned to read and write from teachers she hired to instruct children in her home. Once she had acquired these skills, she taught youngsters the catechism of her beloved Roman Catholic Church.[17] Some of the girls who learned at her knee became teachers themselves. For example, Sophia Bailly, after receiving a liberal education in French, embarked upon a fifteen-year teaching career at St. Ignace. Bailly learned much from her teacher as she circulated freely among the notable visitors to Mackinac, who ranged from Indian chiefs to scholars and from bishops to statesmen.[18] In 1830, Laframboise assisted Father Samuel Mazzuchelli in opening a school for Catholic children on the Island.[19] Soon twenty-six boys and girls were receiving instruction from Martha Tanner and Josephine Marly.

Magdelaine Laframboise

Previous to Tanner's conversion to Catholicism, she had been educated at Ferry's Protestant mission.[20] Laframboise's commitment to self-education helped her to assume a prominent place in the changing society around her. Likewise, her efforts to educate youth helped to prepare them to cope successfully with Americans and their institutions. Some of her students, then, went on to influence still others.

Laframboise was a devout Roman Catholic throughout her life, even though there were no resident priests at Mackinac until 1830. Both she and her husband faithfully prayed the Angelus each day, a practice which Laframboise continued after Joseph's death. At Mackinac, the church bell sounded for the Angelus at six in the morning, at noon, and at six in the evening. The peals caused her to stop work for a moment and repeat the ritual of making the sign of the cross, bowing her head, crossing her hands, and saying short prayers.[21] When, in the 1820s, a site was needed for a new church, Laframboise donated land beside her house.[22] As a token of appreciation, the church relieved her of paying annual pew rental fees and assigned her pew number one.[23] In 1830, when Father Mazzuchelli came to Mackinac to be the first resident priest there since 1765, he lived for a time in Laframboise's home.[24] Her commitment to Catholicism always remained strong, and she used both her time and material resources to further the cause of her church.

Concern for the poor also characterized Laframboise's contributions to her community. Indian Agent Henry R. Schoolcraft noted in 1837 that she provided food for "a poor decrepit Indian woman" who had been abandoned by her relatives.[25] No doubt she repeated this practice often throughout her life, and she willed that it continue after her death by directing that fifty dollars be distributed "to the most Poor of the Island."[26]

Laframboise extended her warm hospitality to Island residents and visitors alike. Editor and critic Margaret Fuller, on a visit to the Island in 1843, gave this account of Laframboise and her relationship to Indian visitors: "The house where we lived belonged to the widow of a French trader, an Indian by birth, and wearing the dress of her country. She spoke French fluently and was very ladylike in her manners. She is a great character among them. They were all the time coming to pay her homage, or to get her aid and advice; for she is, I am told, a shrewd woman of business."[27] English-speaking Americans who resided on the Island also socialized at her home. Gurdon Saltonstall Hubbard remarked that Laframboise's house was one of the places where he and his friends could feel "fully at leisure" on Sunday afternoons.[28] Travellers from the eastern United States and Europe also called upon her and came away impressed with her deportment and sophistication. One such visitor was the French aristocrat, Alexis de Tocqueville. He was pleased to converse with Laframboise in French in order to learn about her Ottawa ancestry.[29]

The wide range of her associates and visitors and the groups of people they represented clearly indicate the esteem which the Mackinac community had for Laframboise. She had a clear sense of her own identity. Unlike many other métis, she not only drew upon the heritage of both her Ottawa and French-Canadian relatives but also successfully came to terms with the newly arriving Americans. She continued to wear Ottawa dress but entertained English-speaking Americans socially and did business with them in the marketplace without feeling out of place even among the new breed of New England fur traders. Her ability to speak all of the languages used at Mackinac, especially English, enabled her to communicate with virtually every person who crossed her path. Her commitment to education for herself, her children, and

Magdelaine Laframboise

the children of her community reveals an understanding of the future. She knew that those in the next generation needed to know how to read and write if they hoped to find a niche in a rapidly changing society. Yet, as she adjusted to and made accommodations for the changing order, Laframboise continued to derive strength and resolve both from Roman Catholicism and from her Ottawa roots. By affiliating herself with the American Fur Company, she insured material prosperity for herself in conducting a business which she knew well. When she opened up her house to the Presbyterian missionary Ferry, she facilitated the establishment of an educational institution for students with cultural backgrounds similar to her own. With Ferry, she saw an opportunity whereby métis and Indian children could receive the intellectual and technical skills which could prepare them for a society quickly coming under the domination of American institutions.

It is impossible to determine with precision how many individual lives were influenced by Laframboise. Her fur-trading activities affected numerous Ottawa, some of them adversely because of the liquor she traded to them.[30] Some métis men earned their livelihood through their employment with her as boatmen. The records do not indicate how many poor and indigent she fed, clothed, and housed, but the number probably was high. The consistency with which she practiced her faith served as an example for other Catholic métis and an inspiration for priests. Perhaps her most lasting contribution to her society came through her commitment to education. She worked tirelessly to provide opportunities for young boys and girls to learn to read and write. Laframboise understood that change, significant change, was occurring in her society, and that both she and the children of Mackinac needed to prepare for it. Her greatest contribution was not her business success but rather her efforts to uplift the poor and to educate the young. She used much of the profit which she earned in the fur trade to improve the welfare of her community.

Laframboise died in 1846. Her last will and the inventory of her estate confirm the interests and concerns which she had throughout her life. First, she directed that she be buried in the church lot according "to the rights and Ceremony of the Roman Catholic Church." Except for the provision for the poor, she left all of her assets to her relatives and friends. Of particular interest is the one-hundred dollars she left to her niece, Marianne Fisher, who for many years taught Ottawa and métis children at Mackinac and Harbor Springs. Laframboise left her house to her granddaughter, Josette Harriet Pierce, but the remainder of her estate went to her son Joseph.[31] Among her possessions were a mahogany side board, two feather beds, and silver tableware, expensive items of quality purchased by profit from her business, yet the inventory of her estate is refreshingly short.[32] This indicates that although she could have afforded many of the material comforts provided by American society in the early nineteenth century, Laframboise resisted the temptations of conspicuous consumption. Instead she chose to live in a comfortable but simple manner.[33] Education, concern for the poor, devotion to family, and faith in God, these nonmaterial aspects of life on Mackinac Island did more to shape her life than did her success in the fur trade. The life of Magdelaine Laframboise has not been forgotten, and her legacy lives on. Her house still stands on Mackinac Island beside Ste. Anne's Church where Catholics worship on the ground which she donated over 160 years ago.

NOTES

[1]Two biographical sketches of Magdelaine Laframboise are David A. Armour's forthcoming biography in Volume 6 of the Dictionary of Canadian Biography and John E. McDowell,

"Madame Laframboise," Michigan History, Vol. 56, No. 4, pp. 271-286; a recent account of the Ottawa in Michigan is James M. McClurken, "Ottawa," in People of the Three Fires: The Ottawa, Potawatomi and Ojibway of Michigan (Grand Rapids: The Grand Rapids Inter-Tribal Council, 1986); a recent analysis of the métis in the northwestern Great Lakes Region is Jacqueline L. Peterson, "Many roads to Red River: Métis genesis in the Great Lakes region, 1680-1815," in The New Peoples: Being and Becoming Métis in North America, ed. Jacqueline Peterson and Jennifer S. H. Brown (Lincoln: University of Nebraska Press, 1985), pp. 37-71.

[2]"Mackinac Register," August 1, 1786, Collections of the State Historical Society of Wisconsin, 1855-1931, (Madison: State Historical Society of Wisconsin), 19:86. Hereafter cited as WHC.

[3]"Mackinac Register," July 11, 1804, WHC, 18:507.

[4]"Mackinac Register," July 7, 1799, WHC, 19:109.

[5]Elizabeth Thérése Baird, "Reminiscences of Early Days on Mackinac Island," WHC, 14:38-39.

[6]David A. Armour, "David and Elizabeth: the Mitchell Family of the Straits of Mackinac," Michigan History, Vol. 64, No. 4, pp. 17-29 and John E. McDowell, "Thérése Schindler of Mackinac: Upward Nobility in the Great Lakes Fur Trade," Wisconsin Magazine of History, Vol. 61, No. 2, pp. 125-143.

[7]For a good discussion of John Jacob Astor's fur trade experience, see Kenneth W. Porter, John Jacob Astor: Business Man (Cambridge: Harvard University Press, 1931).

[8]"American Fur Company Employees - 1818-1819," WHC, 12:162-63.

[9]"American Fur Company Invoices - 1821-1822," WHC, 11:370-77.

[10]George Boyd, "Abstract of Licenses to trade in Indian Country, Sept. 1, 1821-Aug. 31, 1822," Letters Received by the Office of the Secretary of War Relating to Indian Affairs,

1800-1823, Microcopy #271, Roll 4, 1822-1823, National Archives.

[11] Gurdon Saltonstall Hubbard, The Autobiography of Gurdon Saltonstall Hubbard (Chicago: Lakeside Press, 1911), pp. 22-23.

[12] "Donation of Indian Chiefs to Madelon Laframboise," April 28, 1823, Henry S. Baird Papers, State Historical Society of Wisconsin.

[13] Baird, "Reminiscences," p. 40; Louis H. Burbey, Our Worthy Commander: the life and times of Benjamin K. Pierce in whose honor Fort Pierce was named (Fort Pierce, Florida: IRCC Pioneer Press, 1976), pp. 19-35.

[14] Alexis Laframboise to Madame Laframboise, May 8, 1819, Baird Papers.

[15] "Mackinac Register," August 4, 1821, WHC, 19:133.

[16] William M. Ferry, extracts from Journal, November 3, 1823, American Missionary Register, Vol. 5, No. 3, pp. 89-90.

[17] Juliette M. Kinzie, September, 1830, Wau-Bun: The Early Day in the Northwest (Menasha: The National Society of Colonial Dames in Wisconsin, 1948), p. 9; Baird, "Reminiscences," p. 41.

[18] John C. Wright, The Crooked Tree: Indian Legends and a Short History of the Little Traverse Bay Region (Harbor Springs: C. Fayette Erwin, 1917), p. 25.

[19] Mary Ellen Evans, "The Missing Footnote or, the Cure Who Wasn't There," Records of the American Catholic Historical Society of Philadelphia, Vol. 84, No. 4, p. 199.

[20] Samuel Mazzuchelli to Leopoldinen Stiftung, August 25, 1831, University of Notre Dame Archives, University of Notre Dame.

[21] Baird, "Reminiscences," p. 38.

[22] Baird, "Reminiscences," pp. 41-42.

[23] Financial Record Book 1828-1838, Ste. Anne's Catholic Church, Mackinac Island, Michigan.

[24] Evans, "The Missing Footnote...," p. 199.

Magdelaine Laframboise

[25] Henry R. Schoolcraft, August 23, 1837, <u>Personal Memoirs of a Residence of Thirty Years with the Indian Tribes on the American Frontiers...</u> (Philadelphia: Lippincott, Grambo and Co., 1851), p. 569.

[26] Magdelaine Laframboise, Last Will, March 2, 1846, Probate Court Records, Book 1, Mackinac County Court House, St. Ignace, Michigan, pp. 23-24.

[27] S.M. Fuller, <u>Summer on the Lakes in 1843</u> (Iron Mountain: Ralph W. Secord Press, 1985), p. 250.

[28] Hubbard, <u>Autobiography</u>, p. 133.

[29] George Wilson Pierson, <u>Tocqueville and Beaumont in America</u> (New York: Oxford University Press, 1938), p. 302.

[30] McDowell, "Madame Laframboise," pp. 280-81.

[31] M. Laframboise, last will.

[32] Inventory of Magdelaine Laframboise's estate, September 30, 1846. Probate Court Records, Book 1, pp. 29-30.

[33] "Madelaine Laframboise," Account for 1824-1827, American Fur Company Record Books, Account Book Retail Store, 1824-1827, Robert Stuart House, Mackinac Island, Michigan.

SOJOURNER TRUTH (CIRCA 1797 - 1883)

SOJOURNER TRUTH
CRUSADER FOR WOMEN'S RIGHTS

Beverly Ann Fish

Sojourner Truth traveled thousands of miles, spoke before Congress, met two presidents, and was a friend to many of the leading abolitionists, women's rights activists and politicians of her time. Born in slavery, unable to read or write, Truth was to become one of the most famous Black women in American history. By the late 1800s, Truth's life had become a legend. Yet despite her fame, few history books dedicate more than a few sentences to this remarkable woman. Her famous speech, "Ain't I a Woman", is often printed in history texts and feminist anthologies, but little is written about Truth herself. As is often the case with legends, Truth's life has become a mixture of myth and reality. Most history texts describe her only as an abolitionist, although she was much more active for women's rights and was not afraid to link the issues of racism and sexism.

Truth was a firm believer in equal rights for women. Although she wasn't present at the Seneca Falls convention in 1848 when the women's rights movement was formally organized by Elizabeth Cady Stanton and Lucretia Mott, she did attend the Rochester Women's Rights Convention two years later. When she was asked by Harriet Beecher Stowe about her opinions on women's rights, she replied:

Well, honey, I's ben der meetins, an harked a good deal. Dey wanted me fur to speak. So I got up. Says I, 'Sisters, I a'n't clear what you'd be after. Ef women want any rights mor'n deys got, why don't dey jes' take 'em, an' not be talkin' about it?'[1]

The most amazing aspect about Truth's fame is the fact that her life as a public lecturer did not begin until she was over forty years old. Truth often refered to herself as "a self-made woman". Born Isabella, the daughter of slaves in upstate New York, she spent the early years of her life as the slave of John Dumont. In 1817 the New York legislature had passed an Emancipation Act which declared that slaves over forty years old were to be freed and that all would be free on July 4, 1828. Dumont promised Isabella that he would free her one year early if she "would do well and be faithful."[2] When he refused to abide by his agreement, she packed up her few belongings and the youngest of her five children and went to live with the Van Wagoners, a neighboring Quaker family. Although this family was opposed to slavery, they agreed to purchase Isabella so that she would not have to be returned to Dumont. For a year Truth lived with the Van Wagoners as a free servant.

It was during her stay with the Van Wagoners that Isabella discovered the Quaker religion. As a slave, she had not been allowed to read the Bible or to even hear it read. Now she had children read the Bible to her, repeating a passage several times until she had it memorized.[3] Isabella also began to develop her distinctive speaking style during this period. She believed the only way to pray was out loud. She later described her style as, "I talk to God and God talks to me. I goes out and talks to God in the fields and woods."[4]

In 1828 Isabella moved to New York City to work as a domestic and soon became involved in the moral reform movement occurring in the city at that time. The Female Moral Reform Society and the Female Benevolent Society had been organized for the purpose of aiding "fallen women." Through her reform movement acquaintances, Isabella was invited to join the local church. Truth later recalled, "I liked the Quakers but they wouldn't let me sing, so I joined the Methodists".[5]

On June 1, 1843, Isabella decided to change her life. She packed a few belongings, said goodbye to her employer, and set out for the countryside to become a traveling preacher. She also decided to take a new name. She later explained, "I went to the Lord an' asked him to give me a new name. And the Lord gave me Sojourner, because I was to travel up an' down the land, showin' the people their sins, an bein' a sign unto them." Truth became her surname since she was "proclaiming God's truth."[6]

Truth began speaking at many religious revival meetings throughout the New England area. Dressed as a Quaker in dark clothing, she soon gained recognition with her forceful speech and appearance. Ministers gave her letters of reference and sent her from congregation to congregation.

A turning point occurred when she arrived at the Northampton Association in central Massachusetts. Her stay at this commune was to influence the direction of the rest of her life. Formed by David Mack, a friend of Nathaniel Hawthorne, the Association was an experiment in communal living. In the evenings, the members gathered in the parlor to discuss the political issues of the day. At Northampton, Truth met many of the leading abolitionist and women's rights leaders of the era: abolitionists George Benson, Helen Benson Garrison, William Lloyd Garrison, and Samual Hill; David Ruggles, Black secretary of the New York Vigilance Committee and station master of the Eastern Yard of the Underground Railroad; women's rights activists Amy Post and Olive Gilbert.

Post, a station master of the Rochester terminal of the Underground Railroad, began taking Truth to meetings of abolitionists and women's rights organizations. Gilbert was so fascinated by Truth's life that she helped Truth to write her biography, <u>The Narrative of Sojourner Truth, A Northern Slave, Emancipated from Bodily Servitude by the State of New York in 1828</u>.[7]

During her stay at Northampton, Truth listened a great deal and began forming her own ideas about women's rights and the problem of slavery. Truth saw the connection between racism and sexism as similar types of oppression committed by white males. Unlike many of the women's rights leaders and abolitionists, she was not afraid to link the issues. In 1851, Truth's presence at the Women's Rights Conference in Akron, Ohio, caused considerable concern among the women's rights advocates who feared that the association of the two causes would weaken the feminists' position. Many of the women urged the chair of the convention, Frances Gage, not to let Truth speak. Fortunately, Gage personally believed that "temperance, freedom, justice to the Negro, justice to the women are but parts of one whole, one temple whose builder is God."[8] When Truth rose to speak, Gage decided against the opinion of the crowd and permitted her to address the convention. Truth soon won the respect of the audience with her famous speech, "Ain't I a Woman?"[9]

> Dat man ober dar say dat womim needs to be helped over carriages, and lifted ober ditches, and to have de best place everwhar. Nobody eber helps me into carriages, or ober mudpuddles, or bigs me any best place. And a'n't I a woman? Look at me! Look at me arm! I have ploughes and planted, and gathered into barns, and no man could head me! And a'n't I a woman? I could work as much and eat as much as any

man—when I could get it—and bear de lash as well. And a'n't I a woman?

After her success at the Akron Convention, Truth became a regular speaker at women's rights conferences. With her quick wit and her powerful presence, she was not afraid to challenge the hecklers who came to break up the women's conventions. In September 1853, Truth attended the Women's Rights Convention in New York City which was later described as a "mob convention" by the press. For two days, the women speakers had been interrupted by the booing, hissing crowds of men in attendance. On the third day, Truth appeared and shamed the crowd to silence. To their booing and hissing she responded, "Isn't it good for me to come and draw forth your spirit, to see what kind of spirit you're of? I see that some of you have got the spirit of a goose and some of you have got the spirit of a snake."[10]

Wherever Truth went, she had the same impact on the crowds who heard her. She had a quality that appealed to the people and once explained, "I tell you I can't read a book, but I can read the people."[11] She never prepared her remarks but relied on humor and a powerful voice. She prefaced her remarks to an audience in Florence, Massachusetts, with the comment, "Children, I have come here tonight like the rest of you to hear what I have got to say."[12] Harriet Beecher Stowe said of Truth's remarkable style, "I do not recollect ever to have been conversant with anyone who had more of that select and subtle power which we call personal presence than this woman."[13]

Truth was never one to be intimidated by anyone or anything. Because of her powerful speaking manner and her independent spirit, she was often accused of being a man dressed in women's clothing. She put an end to that rumor in

Silver Lake, Indiana, when she exposed her bared breasts to the audience which had accused her.[14]

Women's suffrage was always a priority for Truth. She regretted the fact that there were no women in Congress as she believed that women would be more inclined to promote social welfare issues, such as her proposal of the Western Lands Petition, which would have set aside lands in the west for the Blacks displaced by the Civil War. She was also distressed by the passage of the Fourteenth Amendment of the Constitution which gave Black men the right to vote but ignored any reference to women. While her Black friends, Frederic Douglass and Frances Watkins Harper, argued that since the Blacks had suffered greater hardships they should receive prior consideration, Truth remained loyal to her feminist friends, Susan B. Anthony and Elizabeth Cady Stanton, who continued to assert that "the demand of the hour is equal rights for all."[15] Truth was to later follow Susan B. Anthony's example and try to vote illegally in Battle Creek, Michigan, in the 1872 elections. Unlike the authorities in the Anthony incident, no one dared to arrest Sojourner Truth.[16]

Even when she was over eighty years old, Truth continued to travel and speak at women's rights conferences. Her message was persistence. In 1867 at the American Equal Rights Association Convention, Truth encouraged the women to continue the fight for women's suffrage. She stated, "I am for keeping the thing going while things are stirring; because if we wait til it is still, it will take a great while to get it going again. . . When woman gets her rights man will be right".[17]

Although she had lived in Michigan since 1856, Truth had spent much of her time often on the road. In her later years she spent more time at her home at 10 College Place in Battle Creek, Michigan. Yet she did not completely retire from public life but continued to travel throughout the state speaking on suffrage for women, temperance, and prison reform. In 1878, Truth managed to speak in thirty-six towns in Michigan and to attend a Women's Rights Convention in Rochester, New York.[18]

When Sojourner Truth died at her Michigan home in 1883, over 1,000 people attended her funeral. She had been one of the most admired women of her era. Because of her devotion to women's rights and the issue of equality for all, she brought the ideas of suffrage and social welfare reform before the people of the midwest. She deserves to be remembered as one of America's first Black feminists. As Truth herself proclaimed, she was in the women's movement, for the simple reason that she was, herself a woman.[19]

NOTES

[1] Victoria Ortiz, Sojourner Truth (New York: Lippencott, 1974), p.78.

[2] Olive Gilbert, Narrative of Sojourner Truth, A Northern Slave, Emancipated from Bodily Servitude by the State of New York in 1828 (New York: Arno Press, 1968, reprint), p.39.

[3] Gilbert, p.208.

[4] Gilbert, p.147.

[5] Berenice Lowe, Tales of Battle Creek (Battle Creek: 1976), p.13.

[6] Lowe, p.239.

[7] Gilbert, p. 137.

[8] Ortiz, p. 175.

[9] Gilbert, p. 133.

[10] Ortiz, p.180.

[11] Gilbert, p.216.

[12] Gilbert, p.312.

[13] Gilbert, p.151.

[14] Gilbert, p.139.

[15] Miriam Schneir, *Feminism: The Essential Historical Writings* (New York: Random House, 1972), p.128.

[16] Gilbert, p.231.

[17] Philip Foner, *The Voice of Black America* (New York: Simon and Schuster, 1972), pp. 375-76.

[18] Ortiz, p.233.

[19] Gilbert, p.218.

LAURA SMITH HAVILAND (1808 - 1898)

LAURA SMITH HAVILAND
EMANCIPATOR

Emily Ann Dietrich

Laura Smith Haviland sat in a Toledo hotel, pen poised, trying to think quickly, yet appear calm. She had the distinct impression that the two men standing above her were the slave-holding Chesters. The Chesters wanted her to write a letter to Willis Hamilton and his family, to get them back into their clutches. She had her safety and the Hamiltons' at stake.

The Chesters, who towered above petite Laura Haviland, knew she had tried to trick them by bringing a black student from her school to pose as Willis Hamilton. The Hamilton family had escaped from the Chesters and were living on Haviland's farm. As the Chesters saw it, Haviland was keeping their valuable property from them. In Haviland's view, she was fighting for the Hamiltons' rights as human beings. All three, the two Chesters and Haviland, were serious about this business, but the Chesters had guns.

Haviland forced a smile and said she would gladly write the Hamiltons and tell them to visit their sick friend, whom the Chesters claimed was dying in the next room. She asked the Chesters politely if she might include a few instructions to hasten the Hamiltons' journey. Seeing no harm, the slave-holders agreed. Haviland used the opportunity to warn the freed slaves. She told Elsie Hamilton to get clothes which did not exist from rooms which did not exist, and to get to the train station with a team of horses and a farm wagon, neither of which existed.

The Chesters were not through with Haviland yet. They waited outside her hotel in Toledo and followed her onto the train bound for her home in Michigan. At the first opportunity, the Chesters ran toward Haviland, pointing their pistols in her face. They called her a thief and swore they would kill her. Haviland calmly denied their charges and threats, and finally the Chesters were chased into the woods by angry abolitionists.

Incidents such as this gave Laura Smith Haviland such titles as "that damned abolitionist" and "a rabid abolitionist."[1] She also received the high distinction of having a head worth $3,000 to slave-owners--more than they would pay for a slave![2] She once saw a coal-barge called the "L.S. Haviland," characterizing her as a vehicle by which black cargo was brought north. Her creed was unpopular in the South: she insisted, "Whatever priviledge you claim for yourself, or I claim for myself, I claim for every other human being in the universe, of whatever nation or color."[3]

Even in her own community, Lenawee County, Michigan, Haviland's views made her "a thorn in the side," pricking the conscience of citizens whom she asked for money and supplies to give people oppressed by poverty, ignorance, or slavery.[4] Laura Smith Haviland not only tricked slave hunters, she also started schools, petitioned for the release of prisoners, nursed the ill, bore seven children, relieved the poor, and spread the light of salvation. Her belief in the rights of all people to education, freedom, religion, and simply a roof overhead kept Haviland working and traveling all of her life.

Haviland's belief in these rights was a central part of her life. Unlike many abolitionists, she was not converted to antislavery by the rampant propaganda of the time. Laura

Smith was born Dec. 20, 1808, in what is now Ontario, to Quaker parents, Quakers had been antislavery since before the Revolutionary War. In her childhood, the young girl read and re-read a history of the slave trade by John Woolman, a Quaker. She read how blacks were torn mercilessly from their families in Africa and brutally whipped and beaten when they got to America. She learned how slaves were denied education and religion, both held very important by the Quakers. Antislavery workers had accomplished the halt of overseas slave trade by 1808, the year of Haviland's birth, but there were already almost four million slaves in the United States.[5] Most members of the Society of Friends, as Quaker congregations are called, had already voluntarily freed their slaves at great cost to themselves.

Young Laura Smith had trouble with the Quaker faith itself. The Quakers rejected belief in God which came from "mere excitement"; they emphasized belief that came from knowledge and personal experience.[6] Yet Smith sometimes wanted to sing or pray aloud when she experienced or knew God, like the Methodists or Baptists. She had dreams, visions, and what she called "impressions" which showed her the duty to serve God. The excitement and energy these impressions gave her made Smith reluctant to act on them or to share them with her parents. She even kept her feelings from her husband, Charles Haviland, whom she married in 1823. Her pent-up energy, and her feeling that she was not serving God adequately made her feel "lost...Irretrievably lost!"[7]

Laura Smith Haviland began to find a channel for her energy through the Logan Female Anti-Slavery Society, the first one of its kind in Michigan.[8] She began to understand what her duty was. Ironically, following this duty meant leaving the Quakers of her community. Like many Quaker meetings across the country, her meeting was splitting over the slavery issue. Some Quakers wanted to break the law, committing civil disobedience to help free slaves, while others felt they should wait for God to provide the right moment for freedom.

Laura and her husband, Charles Haviland, decided they would break from their Society of Friends so that they could actively work toward the freedom of the slaves. "We claim a higher law," they wrote to their Society," than the wicked enactments of men who claim the misnomer of law by which bodies and souls of men, women and children are claimed as chattels."[9] The "wicked enactments" were, at that time, part of the Constitution of the United States of America: to accomplish the goals she set for herself and for the universe, Laura Smith Haviland had often to break the laws of men, the laws of her religion, and the laws of convention.

Haviland's first major endeavor broke many conventions. In 1837, the year Michigan achieved statehood, Haviland and her husband started a school called Raisin Institute, named for their small town of Raisin, Michigan. Raisin Institute began as a school for destitute children. Haviland wanted to help young boys and girls be industrious and useful. They brought nine young girls and boys from the poorhouse and taught them farming and sewing. The Havilands hoped to provide these children with education, religion, and the ability to be useful, thus giving them the tools to rise out of the oppression of poverty.

Within two years, the school had expanded into a normal school for teachers or for those who wanted to go on to college. Its purpose was "moral, intellectual and spiritual improvement" for any youth "of good moral character."[10] In 1837, many states had laws prohibiting the education of blacks; people who educated them were persecuted.[11] The new state of Michigan had no such laws, and Raisin Institute admitted both women and blacks, the first school in Michigan to do so. The Haviland's school was in direct competition with the Raisin Seminary, which was run by the Society of Friends they had left. Contemporaries said "If [the Havilands] would give up the vexed abolition question, and let the Negroes alone, Raisin Institute would become the most popular school in the state."[12]

Laura Smith Haviland would never give up the "vexed abolition question." Students who came to her school learned to respect blacks and to work with them. Raisin Institute, in its thirty years of existence, served the needs of black and poor in whatever way was most necessary at the time. Before the war it harbored fugitive slaves and prepared blacks to teach and whites to advocate abolition.

Laura Smith Haviland's husband, Charles, was her partner in this endeavor, but he died in 1845. The rheumatic fever that took him also killed one of their children and almost took Laura Haviland herself. Debts and taxes almost left Haviland and her six remaining children homeless. She felt "in doubts as to [her] ability to get through these rough places of outside life."[13] She accepted charity and depended on God and her "impressions" for support. She finally raised the money for her debts and taxes, but she felt strongly that taxing her, who as a woman had no vote, was tyranny. Laura Haviland's greatest concern was raising her six surviving children, but at the same time she helped escaping slaves and ran the school and the farm.

It was after the death of her husband, when Laura Smith Haviland was 37 years old, that she began her rigorous involvement in antislavery activities with the Hamilton family and the Chesters. The Lenawee community was an ideal place to assist escaping slaves. An often-traveled route on the Underground Railroad begain in Cincinnati, stopped in Lenawee County where Adrian was, and went on to Canada. The Adrian and Raisin community worked hard to protect "self-freed" (escaped) slaves. Abolitionists would ring church bells and blow tin horns to alert the community and the fugitive that a slave hunter was prowling about and do everything they could to get the freed slave to Canada.

Helping fugitive slaves reach Canada had always been dangerous. In 1850, however, the Fugitive Slave Act made protection of escaped slaves not only dangerous, but criminal. In Michigan, state officials were not allowed to help recapture slaves, but slaveholders' rewards tempted many Northerners to join them in finding the slaves.[14] It was hard enough to free slaves; it became even harder to guarantee their freedom.

Many of the fugitive slaves Laura Smith Haviland harbored or helped had to leave their wives and children behind in slavery. Haviland's Underground Railroad missions into slave territory were often undertaken to deliver messages to freedmen's families or to help them plan an escape. Haviland left her school, farm, and family to go to Cincinnati, where her Quaker friend, Levi Coffin, and the "vigilance committee" would help her find ways to deliver these messages and plan routes to freedom. Coffin sometimes reproved Haviland for becoming too involved with particular freed or fugitive slaves, but she had learned to trust her feelings and resolved to help the blacks in any way she could.

The committee directed Haviland's path further south and into further danger, sending her into Kentucky and Arkansas, where the Chesters had posted rewards for her head. Haviland was glad for the opportunity; she wanted to see "more of the system of slavery in its own territory, as so many people of the North were insisting on our exaggerations."[15] Haviland, with her Quaker background, wanted firsthand knowledge of the subject. In Kentucky, she saw what one of the reputed kindest slave owners fed his slaves: sour milk, scraps of pork and rotting greens after they had worked all day. In Arkansas, she stayed with a family who whipped two ten-year-old slaves almost to death because they could not light the fire in the morning.

On these message-bearing missions, as on her mission to save the Hamiltons, Haviland had to invent pretenses to keep herself and the slaves safe. In Kentucky, she posed as someone's aunt and delivered her message to a freedman's sister while pretending to pick berries. In Arkansas, she posed as a seamstress while watching carefully for a sign to meet a freedman's wife. When she arrived at the meeting place, she was met, not by a slave, but by a pack of vicious dogs. Her bold stare in the eyes of the pack's leader made the dogs skulk away, tails between their legs. Haviland produced the same effect on pro-slavery men when she had the opportunity to reveal her antislavery feelings. Her bold stance and confident arguments made the men skulk away.

Haviland not only delivered messages from self-freed slaves to their families, she also helped slaves to free themselves. Many Southerners thought of abolitionists as people who stole slaves or wanted slaves as property for themselves.[16] This was not true of Haviland nor of any abolitionist worthy of the name. She never urged slaves to escape, nor put the idea into their head, but when they suggested to her that they would like to escape, she would try to help them. In Cincinnati, she visited slaves who were hiding while they waited for an opportunity to go north, and there she provided clothes and food to prepare them for their trip.

Haviland used her careful tricks to help get slaves to the North. Once she forged a letter and sent it to Canada and then back to the master of an escaped nursemaid to make him think his slave was permanently out of his clutches. Another time, a young woman was being hidden in a house right between two slave owners. She powdered the fugitive's face so she would appear to be white and wrapped her belongings in a bundle to look like a baby. She and the fugitive walked nonchalantly right past the slave owners. Haviland was always, as she said, "carelessly careful."[17]

Laura Haviland often accompanied fugitives on the full route of their escape. They had to be extremely careful getting out of Cincinnati, where paid slave-hunters swarmed every time news of an escape was heard. The vigilance committee used covered wagons and barges to get the slaves north. These means of transportation cost money which the escaping slaves seldom had. Haviland would have to stop at places along the way to try to get money for the slaves' passage.

Haviland also worked to educate free slaves who had settled in Cincinnati, Toledo, and Canada. Many whites tried to trick the freed slaves in contracts, because they knew the blacks could not read. This made literacy very important. She committed herself to the education of blacks and with her sister opened a school in Toledo in 1852, where they worked for literacy among the freedmen. They viewed inability to read and write as a form of oppression which allowed freedmen to be cheated of money, knowledge, and religion. Haviland also helped to establish a community of freedman in Windsor, Canada, where she founded a church and a school which helped to give blacks confidence in a life of freedom.

In 1861 the Civil War began, putting a halt to the Underground Railroad. The main issue of the Civil War was not necessarily freeing the slaves, but keeping the United States united. Many concessions to slavery had been made in order to make the South willing to remain part of the Union.[18] Even Lincoln did not work full force to free the slaves until well after the Civil War began; he issued the Emanicpation Proclamation in September of 1862. Freedom of the slaves seemed to antislavery workers to be a subordinate issue in the eyes of the government.

Laura Smith Haviland

By 1863, many of Raisin Institute's students had enlisted in the army, so Haviland closed the school and answered the calls from three different organizations needing help for the effects of the Civil War. President Lincoln established the United States Sanitary Commission and called for women of the North to help nurse soldiers.[19] The Christian Commission wanted people to distribute Bibles to the soldiers. The Freedman's Aid Commission wanted to help black war refugees, who were now homeless but not altogether free. Haviland answered Lincoln's call for nurses and the Christian Commission's call for spiritual guidance, but she differed from many women of the time in that her primary effort was to relieve the black families whom the war left homeless and hungry.

Haviland worked for a month gathering supplies, blankets, shoes, clothing, and food. She left her home in Raisin with advice from her son to watch her health, with letters of introduction from Michigan's governor and a state senator, but with only $15.00 in cash. She was 55 years old, but she hoped "the experience of age might make up for the strength of youth."[20] She arrived in Chicago with trunks of supplies and no way to get to Cairo, the southernmost town in Illinois. Many people were flooding to Cairo to try and help their own relatives, so her chances of getting free passage were slim, but something about Laura Haviland's bearing and purpose always helped her succeed on the missions she undertook.[21]

Haviland visited many refugee camps, giving supplies and advice. She often spoke to the freed blacks, saying, "I have come to inquire after the health of this people, body, soul and spirit."[22] She listened to the suffering of those who had been turned out of their homes, who had been beaten, and—this always affected Haviland deeply—separated mercilessly from their families. Many had not even a blanket to keep their half-naked bodies warm. Haviland had to judge quickly what was needed, who needed the most, and how much to give each family. The freed slaves expressed concerns not only that they would be enslaved again after the war, but also that their life as free people would be worse than their lives as slaves: "They say we are free, but what sort of freedom is this with nothing to cover us?"[23] Haviland did her best to show them that their fears were unfounded. Her blankets made them warm, her "forceful and convincing" speeches gave them confidence.[24]

Haviland risked her life and health many times on these missions. Once the barge she traveled on was threatened by Confederate shots. The rivers were very dangerous during the Civil War because weapons and supplies were transported on barges, yet Haviland still traveled on them. Once she drove ten miles in a terrible storm to bring blankets to twenty refugee families. Another time she rode a mule trying to reach a refugee camp. When the mule ran out of control and threw Haviland off, she suffered a concussion.

Haviland also visited many hospitals for wounded soldiers, hospitals that made her "disgust fill to the brim."[25] Thousands of wounded and dying men were lying in fields or abandoned churches. They were fed contaminated soup and operated on in highly unsanitary conditions. Haviland nursed the soldiers herself, but she also worked to make sure they would be under good care because she felt that "every soldier was some mother's son."[26] Once she came across a surgeon in charge of a hospital who was too drunk to do his duty. Haviland got him removed from his post.

Laura Smith Haviland followed faithfully her dream and "impressions," after having suffered for not doing so in her youth, and they almost always guided her truly. She helped prisoners of war as well as wounded soldiers. She had visited a Kentucky prison before the war to try to help a fellow abolitionist, Calvin Fairbanks, whose successful work with fugitives had landed him in jail. There she saw the terrible conditions of the prisons and the injustices done to the prisoners, and she tried to ease Fairbanks' suffering. On a visit to Ship Island in the Gulf of Mexico, Haviland worked to relieve more than fifty prisoners. When she was in New Orleans surveying hospitals, a man requested that she visit Ship Island. Her companion felt they should deny his request, but Haviland "could not rid herself of the impression that it would be right to go."[27] A short while later, they were accidently stranded on Ship Island, an event that was a blessing in disguise. The next day Haviland visited the prisoners, saw their terrible conditions, and found out why they were there. Most of the prisoners were Union soldiers who had been sentenced for life by a Confederate judge for crimes such as drunkenness, suspicious character, and insubordination. Haviland knew that the North needed soldiers, so she cut through the red tape, piece by piece, until she got word from Washington that the whole regiment had been released and were able to return to the war.

After the fighting stopped, Laura Smith Haviland worked to help homeless and uneducated blacks. The Federal Government established an organization for this purpose, the Freedman's Aid Bureau. Its office in Detroit appointed her as a representative. She received the first salary in her life, $40.00 a month, for collecting and distributing supplies. Haviland was determined to help the freed slaves begin their new life in America, not to leave them to struggle alone or to send them to Haiti or Liberia as was Lincoln's plan.[28] In Kansas and Missouri, she set up schools and shelters for white and black refugees. She said of some Southern whites, that "the greatest difficulty in mananging this class was to get them to do anything. Not so with colored people; they would do anything they could find to do."[29] Haviland requested that "no clothing be given to healthy men and women who refused to do work when they could get it."[30]

Haviland sold the Raisin Institute buildings to the State of Michigan in 1865 to be used as the Haviland Home for the Homeless. She traveled to Washington, D.C. to find families who needed Michigan's facility and to survey the aid being given to the many free blacks who had congregated in Washington, thinking they would be safe. She found that she had to badger a soup kitchen manager into serving the blacks the same healthy soup he gave to whites. The Freedman's Bureau was trying to get the power to provide blacks with homes and jobs, but President Andrew Johnson kept vetoing the enabling legislation.[31] As usual, Haviland overcame obstacles in her own way: "We will take these children North where they will be taught habits of industry, as well as to improve their intellects. We of the North think they can learn, if opportunity is provided."[32]

Haviland returned to find her Northern community as unsympathetic to her cause of helping the homeless and poverty-stricken as those in Washington had been. The mothers and children she had sent to her home had never arrived, and there was a letter in her box saying that the destitute people in Haviland Home for the Homeless were becoming an intolerable burden to the taxpayers. Haviland simply could not agree. The next few years of her life focused on raising the children in the home to lead productive lives. She found that almost all residents of prisons had been orphans, and she worked to start a state orphanage, saying "the country poor-houses were but nurseries for prisons."[33] Haviland felt that if young people could be taught to be industrious, they could grow up to be useful members of society, not forced into being criminals. To this end, Haviland petitioned and raised funds for a state orphanage in Coldwater and taught there until it was on firm footing.

Laura Smith Haviland worked against another form of oppression in her sixties. In 1873, the crusade against alcohol, began in Ohio.[34] She brought the temperance crusade to Michigan by closing the seventy saloons in Lenawee County. During that month they were closed, the jails were empty. The temperance movement worked for women whose families were starving because their husbands spent all of their income on alcohol. Women had no rights to property or to their children, and they were powerless to protect their homes. The crusade also involved working for women's right to vote. Haviland thought "that when women were given the ballot, reform movements would be given impetus."[35]

In her later life, Haviland took respite from her toil and travel to write her autobiography, called A Woman's Life Work. Her book devotes as much time to exploring and explaining the evils of slavery as it does to Haviland's own life. She ends the book with a long entreaty to the people of the North to help the freedman. The year was 1881, the slaves had been officially free for almost twenty years, but Haviland insists, "What a misnomer to call our former slave states free!"[36] She reminds Northerners, who even attacked barges so that blacks could not emigrate to the North, that they must help the freed slaves get away from the lynchings and tortures Southerners still inflicted on them. She showed that the Northerners were no more willing than the Southerners to help black people live lives of freedom. When many had forgotten the blacks' trouble, Haviland was still, at 73, collecting supplies, raising money, and starting schools for the freedmen.

Laura Smith Haviland died in 1898, at the age of ninety. Very few conventional histories include her story. Her name appears neither in antislavery books nor in civil war nursing books, but her community remembers her. One of the few statues in the United States honoring a woman was erected to Laura Smith Haviland by Lenawee county citizens. There she sits, in front of Adrian City Hall, poised and content. She seems to be thinking, "Many are the dangers, seen and unseen through which I have passed and this calls forth a renewed song of deliverance and praise."[37] The statue of her is titled, "A tribute to a life consecrated to the betterment of humanity." Haviland's calm look seems to suggest that she believes she had done her duty: she spent her life shining through the darkness of slavery, poverty, and ignorance, shining for the oppressed.

NOTES

[1] Laura Smith Haviland. A Woman's Life Work: Labor and Experiences of Laura Smith Haviland. (Cincinnati: Walden and Stowe, 1882) p. 120.

[2] Harry Ploski, ed. The Afro American: A Reference Work. (New York: Bellweather Company, 1976) p. 12.

[3] Haviland, p. 146.

[4] Dr. Charles Lindquist. Personal Interview: 18, February, 1987.

[5] Bruce Catton. In Richard Ketchum, ed. The Civil War. (New York: American Heritage Publishing Co., 1968) p. 10.

[6] Haviland, p. 6.

[7] Haviland, p. 30.

[8] Dwight Dumond. Anti-Slavery: The Crusade for Freedom in America. (Ann Arbor: University of Michigan Press, 1961) p. 279.

[9] Haviland, p. 93.

[10] Haviland, p. 29.

[11] Ploski, p. 12.

[12] Haviland, p. 35.

[13] Haviland, p. 48.

[14] Ploski, p. 16.

[15] Haviland, p. 215.

[16] Haviland, p. 238.

[17] Haviland, p. 128.

[18]Catton, p. 11-13.

[19]Sylvia G. L. Dannett. Noble Women of the North. (New York: Thomas Yoseloff, 1962) p. 10.

[20]Haviland, p. 243.

[21]Agatha Young. The Women and the Crisis: Women of the North in the Civil War. (New York: McDowell, Oblensky, 1959) p. 151.

[22]Haviland, p. 265.

[23]Haviland, p. 288.

[24]John I. Knapp and R.I. Benner. Illustrated History and Biographical Record of Lenawee County (Adrian: Times Printing Co., 1903) p. 71.

[25]Haviland, p. 258.

[26]Haviland, p. 257.

[27]Haviland, p. 324.

[28]Ploski, p. 16.

[29]Haviland, p. 371.

[30]Haviland, p. 312.

[31]J. G. Randall and David Donald. The Civil War and Reconstruction. (Boston: D.C. Heath and Co., 1961) p. 576.

[32]Haviland, p. 377.

[33]Haviland, p. 438.

[34]Elizabeth Putnam Gordon. Women Torch-Bearers. (Evanston: Women's Christian Temperance Union Publishing Co., 1924) p. 8.

[35]American Association of University Women. Early Adrian. (Swent-Tuttle Press, 1974) p. 83.

[36]Haviland, p. 492.

[37]Haviland, p. 455-6.

LUCINDA HINSDALE STONE (1814-1900)

LUCINDA HINSDALE STONE
CHAMPION OF WOMEN'S EDUCATION

Gail B. Griffin

One of the by-products of traditional historiography, where women are either absent or present only as isolated individuals, is that a woman of accomplishment is likely to be regarded as an anomaly, "ahead of her time." It is the task of the feminist historian not merely to unearth our obscured, distinguished foremothers, but to present them in their historical contexts so they are seen as integral figures in the history of women and not in contrast to the rest of womankind. The remarkable women whom we research and celebrate in this volume serve not only as singular inspirations but also as lenses which allow us to see the more general experience of women at a given historical moment. We should regard these women bifocally, as figures simultaneously exceptional and representative, figures in whose lives we can trace another, larger life, that of Common Woman, who stands for all. Women of accomplishment should be looked at as both exceptional achievers and representatives of the countless unrecognized women of their era.

This double vision is particularly necessary to understand Lucinda Hinsdale Stone. There is no question that she was, by any standards, an extraordinary person--in intellect, learning, courage, energy--or that hers was a life of striking accomplishment, devoted to women's education and progress, accomplishment, devoted to women's education and progress, as many illustrious contemporaries such as Susan B. Anthony warmly attested. By placing her squarely in the nineteenth-century context in which she formed her ideas, especially those concerning women, we enhance rather than diminish her historical significance. Singular as she was, she was very much a woman of her time. As one contemporary put it, "she was one of the best of the Nineteenth Century."[1]

Born on September 30, 1814, to Aaron and Lucinda Mitchell Hinsdale in Hinesburg, Vermont, Lucinda Hinsdale was the last of twelve children. On her father's side, she was descended from French Huguenots and related to the abolitionist-pacifist Elihu Burritt and to Emma Hart Willard, founder of the Troy, New York, Female Seminary, the first endowed institution in the world for the education of women. Through her mother, she was a proud descendent of Anne Hutchinson and a cousin of the astronomer Maria Mitchell, Vassar professor, discoverer (at age twenty-eight) of a comet, and first woman admitted to the American Academy of Arts and Sciences and the Association for the Advancement of Science. This family tree foreshadows most of the major concerns of Lucinda Stone's life.

One other family member merits mention in this regard: her mother, Lucinda Mitchell, age 44 when this last child was born, widowed less than two years later, her life consumed by childbearing and domestic management. She was an avid reader whose lack of educational opportunity haunted her and inspired her daughter, who later wrote, "I have seen her cry oftener for lack of early advantages than for anything else in the world, and she was willing to make any sacrifice for the sake of the education of her own children."[2] Mrs. Hinsdale lamented "the wrong done to the girls of her time . . . . indeed she could never speak of it without tears and with expressing her faith that if God was good and just, as she believed he was, a better time would come for women, though she might not live to see it."[3] Her youngest daughter's life became a pledge to hasten that time.

As a child, Stone was very lonely, fatherless at age two and deprived of the maternal attention her harried mother could not spare her, but, at least in later life, she seems to have seen this deprivation in light of the conditions of domestic life for women and to have viewed her mother with pity and empathy. She lavished on young women the maternal attention she had lacked, and in her work for women's education, she fought to redeem her mother's life. From her father, though she barely remembered him, she took a fairly radical tendency in religious matters—a hatred of sectarianism and of the doctrine of hell—which was to be central to her adult thinking and to her political trouble with the Baptists of Kalamazoo in the 1860's.

Thanks undoubtedly to her mother, Stone received a remarkably good education for a girl of her time. She began grammar school at three, her schoolwork supplemented by extensive home reading. At 13 she entered the new Hinesburg Academy, which had quickly gained a superior reputation. It was also coeducational by the standards of the day: most classes included both sexes, and the college preparatory curriculum, though designed for university-bound boys, admitted girls. At 15 she took her first teaching post, at a nearby summer school, and for a time she transferred to a female seminary in Middlebury, where she also taught French. It was there that she first experienced the inferior standards and pedagogy of an exclusively female institution and became convinced of the necessity of coeducation to insure educational equity and women's progress.

Back at Hinesburg and encouraged by a sympathetic teacher, Stone entered the college preparatory classes with the young men. At the time no collegiate institution existed for women. Oberlin College, in 1833, would be the first in the world to admit black and white students of both sexes, and Mary Lyon's Mt. Holyoke Female Seminary would not open until 1837. Stone's passionate wish was for a college education. Her favorite subject was Greek, a language belonging to the male curriculum and symbolizing cultural tradition and the realms of knowledge reserved exclusively for men. The relentless ridicule she endured from classmates and townspeople because of her aspirations scarred her deeply and galvanized what she later called "an irrepressible desire for the higher, more thorough, college education for women, which should cure the affectation and pettiness of school girls,--in short, give them something worthy to live for and to do for others."[4]

She found sympathy for this heresy in the new principal at Hinesburg, James Andrus Blinn Stone. He was four years her senior, a Middlebury graduate devoted, as she was, to classical studies and languages, and gripped, as she was, by the social and intellectual currents of the day, notably feminism and abolitionism. "It was very evident to the other students," wrote a fellow pupil, "that Mr. Stone was much attracted to Miss Hinsdale."[5]

They were separated for the next four years, while he attended Andover Theological Seminary and she taught briefly at the Burlington Academy before going south to Natchez, Mississippi, to become a governness. There she saw the horror of slavery firsthand--in fact, among her first sights en route to the plantation where she was to work was a young black woman on the auction block, an image she never forgot.

Several of her numerous older siblings had moved west, and in 1840 James Stone joined Lucinda Hinsdale at her sister's home in Grand Rapids, Michigan, where they were married on June 10. Before returning to Gloucester, Massachusetts, where Dr. Stone had taken a ministry, they stopped in Kalamazoo, where he preached at the Baptist Church. He must have made an impression, for three years later he was called back as Principal of the Baptist-controlled Kalamazoo Branch of the University of Michigan.

Two years earlier, in 1841, the Baptist Kalamazoo Literary Institute (formerly the Michigan and Huron Institute, founded in 1833) had merged with one of the eight statewide "branches," preparatory schools designed to create a qualified clientele for the university in Ann Arbor. One of their other functions, however, was to provide "female departments" for young women, who were barred from the university. Suddenly Lucinda Stone, mother of one young son and pregnant with another, was called upon to become Principal of the Female Department of the Kalamazoo Branch. She had not intended to teach, but she found herself at a young, malleable institution, desperately in need of her talent, full of potential, and less trammelled by the traditions and prejudices of the conservative East. She never looked back.

The Stones' 20 year administration of what became Kalamazoo College was epochal in the college's development and in the history of Michigan education. It was truly a joint endeavor, in the minds of students, faculty, and townspeople, though Dr. Stone was officially president and Mrs. Stone took no salary. The aims and efforts of this dynamic team were identical: to bring the college a reputation for superior instruction, to build it into a quality educational institution rather than a narrowly denominational school, to open it to the compelling issues and personalities of the day, and, finally, to subvert as much as possible the nominal separation of the sexes and the curricula, establishing coeducation de facto if not de jure. In all these aims, they were spectacularly successful. By the time the college was chartered as Kalamazoo College in 1855, they had tripled enrollment and forged a curriculum of quality.

Its reputation grew quickly, and the Stones' house on the hill overlooking West Main Street became a sort of cultural center between Detroit and Chicago. "We were openly anti-slavery...and acknowledged woman suffragists, as were most of those who filled the lecture platform in those days," Stone remembered, "and toward the private hotel on the hill people of this kind drifted."[6] They included Elizabeth Cady Stanton, Frederick and Helen Douglass, Bronson Alcott, Wendell Phillips, and Ralph Waldo Emerson. The Female Department thrived, acquiring prestige as a demanding, exciting, and encouraging place of study for young women, who were taught there, as one alumna put it, "that life was earnest, and women had a place to fill, a work to do, as well as men (and a woman) must act well her part."[7]

Both Stones were legendary teachers, but Mrs. Stone's impact on the Female Department was especially profound. Her teaching of her own specialties—English and French literature and Moral Philosophy—was inspired, infused with her philosophy of life as a constant evolution and a high art. The alumnae particularly cherished her Friday talks, in which she spoke informally on some issue of concern to her. In her teaching, she freely combined established authors with contemporary writers, including women such as the Bronte sisters and Elizabeth Barrett Browning. Believing, with other pioneers in the field, that teaching was a natural career for women, she avowed that "the motherheart must be at the center of all true teaching."[8] Indeed, her classroom "appeared like a lot of girls having a friendly talk with their mother, yet never was teaching more effective."[9] The domesticity of the scene was perhaps enhanced by the presence of Prince, the Stones' dog, and Jim, their third son, who sat on his mother's lap as she conducted her classes.

Stone rigorously trained and carefully nurtured her assistant teachers. She developed in them a deep concern for teaching as a profession—one which, during this time, was becoming rapidly feminized as thousands of middle-class women flooded the only viable non-domestic career open to them, particularly on the western frontier. On Saturday evenings, Stone conducted classes for her assistants in an effort to combat what she saw as the potential for exhaustion and stagnation in a teacher's—especially a female teacher's—life. These classes began to incorporate community women, for whom separate courses in history, art, and literature evolved. This development grew into the achievement for which Stone was best known throughout the state and the nation, her leadership in the women's club movement. In 1852 she was one of eight women who constituted themselves the Ladies Library Association, a group which for many years provided the only library in Kalamazoo. This group was one of the first women's clubs in a movement that was to sweep the country in the next fifty years.

In the early 1860s, the tide turned for the Stones at Kalamazoo College, leading them to depart from the school in circumstances of intense hostility, political intrigue, and scandal. The episode seems to have begun with a change in the leadership and philosophy of the Baptist Church, which still controlled the college. Long distinguished by its liberalism and respect for individual conscience, the official church in this decade became narrower, more restrictive, and more conservative. The root cause of the resultant campaign against the Stones was probably their religious progressivism and undisguised resistance to what Mrs. Stone called "religious cant and long-faced Pharisaical religion or its pretense."[10] According to her, the Baptists' minister, Samuel Haskell, aspired to the college's presidency. Suddenly Dr. Stone's leadership and ethics were impugned, while Mrs. Stone's advanced methods and materials were criticized: her use of morally suspect modern novelists and writers such as Byron, her affinity for French language and culture, her familiarity with radical German philosophy, even her subscriptions to contemporary periodicals. The Stones' feminism, including their commitment to coeducation, also met with hostility.

On November 5, 1863, Lucinda and James Stone tendered their resignations. The student reaction was overwhelming: of 194 total students, some 75 per cent withdrew from the college, though many returned the next fall.[11] To meet severe financial exigency, Mrs. Stone opened a female seminary in her own home. The new school naturally drew a large number of former Kalamazoo College students, posing a threat to the institution. Anti-Stone forces retaliated with what all modern accounts agree was a campaign of slander designed to drive the Stones out of Kalamazoo. Their tactic was a series of assaults on Dr. Stone's sexual conduct, alleging involvement with students and with a former servant. Dr. Stone was tried by the church and excommunicated, though he won a civil suit against one of his accusers. In a separate action, Mrs. Stone was also expelled from the church, on grounds of "injurious words against a brother,"[12] that is, Haskell, who, she said, "had cherished toward me, for years, a particular dislike, as one of the class termed 'smart' or literary women."[13] One of her charges against him was his refusal to allow church women a vote in the proceedings, a reversal of long-standing Baptist policy.

The harrowing year-long struggle left the Stones financially and spiritually exhausted and engendered a bitterness which remained with Stone for the rest of her life. It tested the limits of her courage and resiliency, and it was the trial-by-fire that tempered and solidified her character. "To the dark spirits more than to the bright and prosperous days I think we should acknowledge we are indebted for the best of all we know," she later said.[14] "They are what has made me what I am."[15] Exiled from Kalamazoo College, she did more than anyone save her husband to build for the future, conducting school in her home for two years, until it burned in 1866. Now bereft of a classroom, she began to conceive a broader educational mission to women. "I became," she wrote, "what might be called a teacher at large."[16]

Her initial project in this new role was the first of eight trips overseas with a class of young women. She continued these foreign study tours until she was seventy-four, introducing her pupils not only to the art, architecture, and history of Europe and the Middle East, but also to contemporary social structures and problems abroad, including the lives of working people and the roles of women.

In the late 1860s, another project came to fruition. Since 1855 the Stones had been in the forefront of the effort to open the University of Michigan to women, lobbying the state legislature, the university regents, and successive presidents of the institution. Since its charter made eligible "all persons resident of this state," the argument hinged on one of the central issues of the national suffrage movement--that is, whether or not women were legally "persons." For 15 years the battle wore on. Several women applied and were denied, and Alice Boise, a Kalamazoo Branch pupil and the daughter of a University of Michigan faculty member, had unofficially audited classes in Ann Arbor, the first woman in the university's classrooms. But as the 1860s closed, the balance shifted in favor of reform. The Stones convinced a friend among the university's regents of the equity of their cause, and he persuaded his brethren to pass the resolution opening admission to women. Meanwhile, Lucinda Stone had persuaded one of her star pupils to apply as a test case. She was Madelon Stockwell, alumna of both Kalamazoo and Albion Colleges. She was informed that she would be permitted to take the entrance examinations, which she passed. Her admission to the university sent shock waves through the academic world. Although several separate women's colleges were now established, coeducation was still regarded as a highly radical venture, particularly at a large, prestigious state university. Stone later wrote of her protege', "She was the first one to break the ice of an old, old prejudice, and I thank God that I helped her to do it."[17]

In 1890 the University of Michigan awarded Lucinda Stone an honorary doctorate, the second it had granted a woman, but her pressure for coeducation did not let up. During the next decade, she led a campaign to endow a professorship specifically reserved for a woman, believing that "an institution is not really co-educational until it is co-educating--until men and women both and together form the teaching force and influence of that institution..."[18] Significantly, from a biographical viewpoint, she wished the endowment to create "a memorial professorship to our mothers, who longed to see the intellectual sunlight of our day and died without the sight."[19] This particular campaign did not succeed, but it undoubtedly helped clear the way for Dr. Eliza Mosher to become, in 1896, the first woman on the university faculty.

The most enduring of Stone's projects as "teacher at large" was her role as "Mother of Women's Clubs" in Michigan. From Kalamazoo the club concept spread throughout the state as it was spreading across the country. When she was not abroad, Stone was constantly on the road, helping to organize a new club or speaking for an established one. She helped to found Frederick Douglass Clubs for black women and men. When the national General Federation of Women's Clubs came into being in 1890, she became Corresponding Secretary for Michigan. She served on the Michigan Federation's Board of Directors and was later elected honorary vice-president of the national organization. She saw the Kalamazoo Ladies Library Association move into its splendid quarters on Park Street, the first building in the country built by and for a women's organization. While the press ridiculed the club movement as "the Middle-Aged Woman's University," Stone took this phrase seriously.[20] For her, that was precisely what it was.

In 1883, three hundred of the Stones' former pupils converged upon Kalamazoo for a reunion to honor their teachers, an affirmation of the glory days before the debacle of 1863-1864. The Stones were now away from Kalamazoo a great deal; in addition to the foreign travel and trips to out-of-state conferences, Stone and her husband made frequent visits to the families of their sons, Clement in Saginaw and Jim in Detroit. Their middle son, Horatio, had died in 1870. In late 1887 and early 1888, Lucinda Stone endured two major losses: son Clement, and then, seven months later, her husband. She sustained very warm relations with Jim, her surviving child, and with her five grandchildren.

In the 1880s and 90s, her activity seemed to increase. In addition to the major projects described earlier, she wrote voluminously for various Michigan newspapers and for national periodicals such as *The Woman's Journal*, describing lessons drawn from her travels and addressing issues of concern to women. She became a charter member of the Michigan Women's Press Association. She was extremely involved in events during the Chicago World's Fair in 1893, where her picture was part of the Michigan exhibit in the remarkable Women's Building, a monument, as she saw it, to the growing influence and accomplishment of women internationally. During the fair's Congress of Women, she joined Julia Ward Howe and other luminaries on the platform, representing the General Federation of Women's Clubs. In 1894 she became a great-grandmother, and two years later she attended the National Congress of Mothers in Washington D.C. There she mused on the escalating Cuban-American crisis, wishing for "some wise mother-hearts" among the governmental decision-makers. "And there will be sometime," she consoled herself, with her usual faith in women's inevitable progress.[21]

At home in Kalamazoo, she was centrally involved in the establishment and the life of People's Church. After her tangle with the Baptist hierarchy, she had turned to the Unitarians as a less creed-bound and more socially conscious spiritual community. Caroline Bartlett Crane, the church's powerful and controversial minister, became an intimate friend. The last decades of Lucinda Stone's life were also distinguished by friendships with two remarkable black women: Sojourner Truth, who visited her in Kalamazoo and whom she visited in Battle Creek until Sojourner's death there in 1883; and Helen Douglass, Frederick's widow and an activist in the anti-lynching crusade.

Stone always kept in close touch with the national women's suffrage movement. In 1891 she lobbied state legislators to pass a bill enfranchising women in municipal elections, part of the localized strategy adopted by the national leadership as the fight for the Nineteenth Amendment dragged into its fourth decade. Rachel Avery, Mary Livermore, and Michigan's Anna Howard Shaw, all second-generation leaders in the National American Woman Suffrage Association, were correspondents, as were the significant figures of the first generation, Elizabeth Cady Stanton and Susan B. Anthony, who both visited Kalamazoo. On the occasion of Stone's 80th birthday, Anthony wrote: "Please tender to Mrs. Stone my loving and honoring appreciation of her great work for women; not only Michigan women, but the women of the nation and the world owe her very much for her persistent efforts to secure the perfect equalities of educational opportunities for girls."[22]

The last surviving letter to Stone, from Rachel Foster Avery of the National American Women's Suffrage Association, invites her to Anthony's own 80th birthday celebration on

February 15, 1900, but by that point Stone was not strong enough to travel. On March 13, surrounded by family in her Kalamazoo home, she slipped into unconsciousness. Caroline Bartlett Crane spent the night by her side. Shortly after 9:30 the next morning, Lucinda Hinsdale Stone died.

At their biennial convention that year, the General Federation of Women's Clubs passed a resolution honoring "one of the foremost workers of the age and one who made an impress on the life and thought of her time not exceeded by any other woman."[23]

Lucinda Stone's historical importance and modern reputation rest upon three major projects: her role in the history of Kalamazoo College, her work on behalf of coeducation, and her women's club work in Michigan and throughout the nation. It is important that these efforts be understood today as she understood them always, as dimensions of her single great project--the higher education of women. This she regarded as the critical factor in a still larger historical development: "this rising tide of womanly energy" on many different fronts which would eventually revolutionize the world.[24]

Her part in creating Kalamazoo College was the first great work of her life. The college's present status--as the oldest institution of higher learning in the state, respected for academic excellence, innovative programming, and concern for the total personal development of its students--can be traced to the ideals established by the Stone's and nourished by them for twenty years.

Lucinda Stone's leadership in the coeducation movement is extremely significant in the history of women's education. Colleges and universities of the Midwest played a central and unique role. Women's education in the East generally followed the pattern of separate female institutions, while in the Midwest, a combination of economic reality and frontier liberalism generated coeducational schools. They were regarded with alarm by traditionalists but seen by feminists as the real hope for genuine educational equity and for training of women in new roles. We today can scarcely comprehend the degree of controversy surrounding the issue in the nineteenth century. It was central to the whole "Woman Question" because it raised the issues of women's essential nature, abilities, and roles, as well as of the fundamental differences between the sexes. Indeed, it generated speculation about the future of the family and of society itself. Historian Eleanor Flexner has written that by 1865, in the course of this debate, "the higher education of women had made little progress except in the Middle West."[25] The gradual evolution of coeducation which characterized colleges like Kalamazoo, no less than the more overt public battles at state universities like Michigan's, was a means by which women made their way into the male bastions of academe. Lucinda Stone was at the forefront of both battles in Michigan and involved in the national movement through her writings, joining the chorus which demanded for women the freedom of their minds as the first requisite in their long crusade for full citizenship and humanity.[26]

It is noteworthy that Lucinda Stone viewed the admission of women to male institutions as only the first step in coeducation. Her inclusion of material by and about women in her curricula; her care for the development of women teachers; her demand for women in the professorate and other higher echelons of academe--"women on the faculty,....women from the foundation up, women on the board of regents, women who will see what women need, as men can never see it--"; all these concerns show her deep understanding of a problem still with us. She saw the importance of making academic institutions not merely open, but congenial, to women, and of making women fully present in the academic world by insuring that their influence be felt at all levels in all areas.

Meanwhile, she wrote, "while the world has been discussing the question of where women may properly be educated...women themselves...have, by the thousands, and tens of thousands in our country, laid out for themselves elective, or what we have termed 'post-graduate' courses of study which they are pursuing in associations which they call 'clubs,' and which, more than Vassar, and Smith, and Wellesley colleges, are the real institutions at present educating American women."[28] Her half-century of organizing and sustaining women's clubs was, to her, merely the logical continuation of her efforts to open colleges to women. "The women who lacked early opportunities and who hungered for knowledge," wrote her friend and biographer Belle Perry, "appealed to Mrs. Stone in a way which would be difficult for one to understand who did not know her closely."[29] This special appeal drew from her memory of her mother, from her ideal of life as constant growth, and from her joy in seeing women collaborate for their own advancement. Her role as "Mother of Women's Clubs" in Michigan puts her at the center of the first continuing education program for women, a movement important in the social history of the United States because it brought together women who may have had no other vehicle for overcoming barriers between them to join forces, escape the confines of the home, and improve themselves and their communities.

Through the clubs, Mrs. Stone saw her work on behalf of younger women extending outward into society and across the nation, converging with and strengthening the larger tide of woman-energy which distinguished what Victor Hugo called "the Woman's Century." One element of nineteenth-century American feminism was the belief--conservative and radical at once--that the special moral energy of women and their traditional strengths as bearers, nurturers, and preservers of life could be catalyzed by educational, political, economic, and social reform and thus liberated into the stream of human civilization. To Lucinda Stone and other feminists, all the multifaceted efforts to free women were working to create a New Woman, "the woman that is to be." Her function was virtually messianic: "she will come in the fullness of her time, when the world is ready for her—'To serve the world raised up.'"[30] In Stone's words, the struggle to prepare the way for the new woman had already sparked "a new Pentecost in our midst, teaching men of this age something, as the unbelieving Peter was taught in another age, that men and women belong to the same category of human beings and that women are not necessarily bent on mischief when they come together under pretext of seeking to ameliorate some of the ills that in weighing, alas, most heavily on many classes of their own sex, must so much hinder the real advancement of all the common human family."[31] Lucinda Stone's life work is a diverse expression of a feminism which belongs to her own time and speaks eloquently to ours, advocating the freedom of women for their own sakes and also for the sake of a transformed humanity.

NOTES

[1]Lucy Andrews, quoted in the Kalamazoo Evening Telegraph, January 30, 1903. Kalamazoo Public Library collection, hereafter referred to as KPL.

[2]Belle M. Perry, Lucinda Stone, Her Life and Reminiscences (Detroit: Blinn Publishing Co., 1902), p.5.

[3]Letter to T.W. Palmer, July 2, 1891. KPL.

[4]Quoted in Perry, p. 30.

[5]Quoted in Perry, p. 47.

[6]Quoted in Perry, p. 309.

[7] Julia McNair Tenney, Reunion of Former Pupils of Rev. J.A.B. Stone, D.D., and Mrs L.H. Stone (Kalamazoo: Kalamazoo Publishing Co., 1886), p. 100.

[8] Quoted in Perry, p. 341.

[9] A former pupil, quoted in the Kalamazoo Gazette, March 5, 1900. KPL.

[10] L.H. Stone, An Episode in the History of Kalamazoo College: A Letter to Hon. J. M. Gregory, L.L.D. (Kalamazoo, 1868), p. 21.

[11] Charles T. Goodsell and Willis F. Dunbar, A Centennial History of Kalamazoo College (Kalamazoo, 1833), p. 71.

[12] Stone, p. 56.

[13] Stone, p. 24.

[14] Tenney, p. 39.

[15] Lucinda Stone, autobiographical fragment, KPL.

[16] Tenney, p. 44.

[17] Kalamazoo Morning Gazette, July 7, 1899. KPL.

[18] Lucinda Stone, "An Open Letter to the Regents of Michigan University," KPL.

[19] "Club Talks," April 7, 1890. KPL.

[20] Mary I. Wood, History of the General Federation of Women's Clubs (NY: General Federation of Women's Clubs, 1912), p. 26.

[21] Quoted in Perry, p. 157.

[22] Quoted in Perry, p. 157.

[23] Quoted in Wood, pp. 133-34.

[24] "Club Talks," November 5, 1881, KPL.

[25] Eleanor Flexner, Century of Struggle: The Woman's Rights Movement in the United States (NY: Atheneum, 1972), p. 122.

[26] For a fuller discussion of the history of women's education in the midwest, see Gail Griffin, "A Desire to Know: Women's Education in the Midwest," Change, vol. 16, No. 1, January-February, 1984, pp. 32-40.

[27]"Club Talks," April 8, 1894. KPL.

[28]"Club Talks," April 4, 1883. KPL.

[29]Address to the Michigan Federation of Women's Clubs, October 2, 1900; reprinted in Lucinda Stone, Her Life and Reminiscences, p. 183.

[30]Anna C. Brackett, ed., The Education of American Girls (NY: G. Putnam's Sons, 1974), p. 208.

[31]"Club Talks," October 28, 1881. KPL.

No photograph available.

MARION MARSH TODD (1841 - 1914)

MARION MARSH TODD
POPULIST WRITER AND ACTIVIST

Pauline Adams and Emma S. Thornton

Historians have not traditionally associated Populism, the movement rising from economic, political, and social discontent in the latter years of the nineteenth century, with the state of Michigan. Yet a closer scrutiny reveals several Michigan women who were recognized nationally for their efforts on behalf of the Populist cause. Marion Marsh Todd was one of these women. Her tool was her pen, a tool she used with style and acumen in writing both political tracts and sentimental novels. Todd typifies the nineteenth century woman activist with her energetic involvement in public life and voluminous bibliography.

Though born in Plymouth, New York, in 1841, she lived most of her life in Michigan. She was the daughter of a Universalist minister, Abner Kneeland Marsh, and Dolly Wales Marsh. The couple moved their seven children to Eaton Rapids, Michigan when Marion was ten. She attended Ypsilanti Normal School and then taught until her marriage in 1868 to Benjamin Todd, a lawyer from Boston. The Todds had one daughter, Lulu. In the late 1870s they moved to San Francisco where Marion enrolled in Hastings Law College. Her husband died in 1880 and the following year she withdrew from law school without a degree but gained admittance to the state bar. Like many women lawyers at that time, she became politically active even though she had no vote. In 1882 she ran for state attorney general on the Greenback-Labor ticket; though she lost, she led her ticket in votes.

By 1886, Todd had returned to Michigan. She continued to work in reform politics: as a delegate to the Knights of Labor General Assembly in Richmond, Virginia; as a co-founder of the Union Labor Party in 1887; and as a lecturer for political reform. In 1890 she moved to Chicago to edit the Chicago Express, a nationally circulated reform weekly. She soon returned to Michigan, living in Eaton Rapids, Hillsdale, and Springport. A record of her death has not been found, but it occurred about 1914.

Between 1886 and 1902, Marion Marsh Todd authored eight books, five on critical political issues and three novels. An analysis of her works leads to the conclusion that the quality of her five political tracts exceeds that of her later fictional efforts. Each of those political tracts dealt with one of the major problems identified by the Populists—problems that became political issues: the protective tariff, the currency question, the railroad industry, and women's rights.

The title of her first book, Protective Tariff Delusions, describes its contents. The delusions which she exposed were several. According to Todd, Protectionists claimed the protective tariff brought a greater amount of wealth to the nation, greater productivity, higher wages, increased immigration, a home market for the farmer, and better prices for farm produce. She used all the techniques of nineteenth-century rhetoric to prove them wrong: both relevant and irrelevant arguments, statistics, case studies, quotations, even philosophical reflections. She concluded that protective tariffs were a form of class legislation that benefitted only millionaires.

Protection to America has enabled a few men to extend their clutches, until, today, we find ourselves a nation of paupers, presided over by a few millionaires; until today, we find a handful sitting upon their throne of special privileges, gazing with fiendish appetites over the triumph of their harvest...[The resulting] poverty is the mother of crime, and our almshouses and penitentiaries were never as full as now.[1]

At another point, when discussing class division, poverty, and crime, she noted that these problems bring "us face to face with the great need for a more extended market in which to trade,"[2] and, she therefore proposed free trade as a remedy.

Todd's next two books were Honest(?) John Sherman or a Foul Record (1890) and an elaboration of that work, Pizarro and John Sherman (1891). In those books, the culprit responsible for social ills was the scarcity of money in circulation. Her arguments and methods were similar to the ones used in Protective Tariff Delusions. The nation was in an unhealthy state. The cause was "class legislation" which limited the supply of money; hence it benefitted the creditor and hurt the debtor. The major victimizer was Senator John Sherman and the real victim was America. In all three books, it is clear that Todd was convinced that by legislative fiat American could be cleansed just as by legislative fiat it had been befouled.

Todd's chief oeuvre was Railways of Europe and America, published in 1893 with a second edition in 1895. More research, more time, more thought, and more careful documentation went into the writing of this book than into any of her others. She presented tables comparing aspects of the 1890 American and European railway industries: equipment, stock, trackage, workers, accident records, passenger and freight rates. She concluded from the assembled facts that "[railroad magnates] know no people, no party, no God—but the God of Greed, based upon unrighteous dividends and watered stock."[3] "Whether the Railways shall own the people or the people own the Railways" was the question she posed for herself in this book.[4] Her answer was clear: nationalize the American railroad industry.

These four books focus on the economic sector of America in the late nineteenth century. The issues Todd confronted were significant—the Protective tariff, the currency question, railroad abuses. Her analysis was typically Populist, and her recommendations were consistent with the People's Party Platform of 1892. Todd was a lawyer and her form of argument was reminiscent of the techniques fictional courtroom lawyers use to discredit witnesses. She put forth all arguments, great and small, appropriate and inappropriate, logical and intuitive, hoping that her readers would be persuaded somewhere along the line. Persuasion, she believed, would activate the voters to elect better people to public office, out of which would come a better America.

The place of women in American society consumed as much of Todd's attention as did the economy. Thus, when Professor Goldwin Smith, a noted historian at Cornell University, attacked women's suffrage in print, Todd reacted quickly, vehemently, and amusingly in a book called Professor Goldwin Smith and His Satellites in Congress.

Professor Smith had argued as follows: women's suffrage means handing over the government to women. But government is really the domain of men. Government requires the "robustness" and "muscle" of men, not the "tenderness and purity" of women. Voting is not a natural right inherent in all human beings. "Suffrage is not a right but a privilege," and women, being the "angelic portion of humanity" are unfitted for the political struggle. Thus, he said, "If government requires masculine understanding or temperament and if the practical character by which political questions are to be best settled resides in man, whose sphere is the world, rather than in woman, whose sphere is the home, that is the reason for preferring such government and legislation, quite independent of any invidious comparisons whether intellectual or moral."[5] Smith concluded: "To man, as he alone could enforce the law, the sovereign power came naturally and righteously."[6]

Todd parried Professor Smith's thrusts. She seized a word, like "robustness," from Smith's essay and made it a topic for an entire chapter in her rebuttal. She teased it, mauled it, played with it, chewed it. When she finished, the reader would have found it difficult to take Smith's contentions seriously. Over and over again she repeated this process, using anecdotes, newspaper accounts, quotations, biblical allusions, arguments, even history, in playing her game. At times she asserted, echoing Elizabeth Cady Stanton. that woman's "moral status in nature exceeds that of man."[7] For the most part, however, she was remarkably modern in her feminist views. For example, she believed that liberation for women also meant liberation for men. "For women not to demand [equality], is not to be cultured, and for our women not to be cultured is woe unto the race of men."[8] She expanded on this idea, writing not only about equal suffrage, but about equal wages in the workplace. Despite the past "enslavement of women," she was confident that women's suffrage was inevitable "according to the order of progress." "Yes," she affirmed, "it belongs to women to render [justice] to the present and rising generations as can only be rendered by freedom's environments."[9]

In her paean to women's rights, she deconstructed many of the myths, myths still alive today. With style and sometimes humor, she ridiculed Smith's sexist assertions. She was genuinely concerned for the struggling men and women on the fringe of contemporary America. All her political tracts grew out of the exciting and hopeful political climate of the late 1880s and early 1890s when the People's Party (also known as the Populist Party) was at its peak. Activists like Marion Marsh Todd were convinced that they were on the verge of seizing sufficient political power to accelerate human progress. Thus, in her earlier work she relied on the political process to effect change, but by the last half of the 1890s, the People's Party had disappeared. Todd adapted to this change by switching to novels instead of political tracts in order to stir her readers to action. As did many Populists, she abandoned the political process and turned to different arenas. She replaced the specifics of railroad abuses, protective tariffs, scarce money, and women's suffrage with the more abstract concerns of spiritual growth, personal integrity, justice, and compassion for the poor.

Todd wrote an introduction to her first novel wherein she established her reason for writing fiction.

> The common novelist studies to lay plots and present plausible situations, while reality, more terrible and touching with no impossible situations, is oftener unwritten and unknown.
>
> Our standard romance writers picture both real and ideal life, thus in a measure they become the historians of the customs, habits, thoughts and progress of a race. The realistic fiction of a Zola may shock the reader, but if the lesson gleaned excuses its existence, the same apology may be offered in the publicity of reality.
>
> If by drawing attention to the tales of living woe, one heart softens and understanding quickens, creating a

resolve to help change conditions for the betterment of God's children, an useful lesson will have been taught.

To present a few hitherto unwritten lessons is my purpose. In the face of existing situations the propriety of so doing will hardly be questioned, though facts may shock and cheeks may burn.

There are living pictures which should be framed and placed upon the walls of every home, as a supplication to the world.

There is a world within a world today asleep. There are churches loudly preaching Christ that shamefully lack his spirit. There are stratas of society with no heart for humanity. The greed of wealth is abroad in the land, and the hungry wolf growling at the door of the poor. Thus we must write.[10]

Except for a brief segment, her first novel, Rachel's Pitiful History, is inaccessible today and historians are forced to rely on a secondary report of its content. According to Paul L. Murphy in his entry on Todd in Notable American Women, Rachel's Pitiful History, published in 1895, was a novel of "political and social protest, lachrymosely chronicling the tragedy of human exploitation and debauchery, which she blamed on the capitalist system, and criticizing the churches for their hypocrisy in not rising to their social responsibilities."[11] Though her first and second novel are unobtainable, her third and final novel, Claudia, published in 1902 and dedicated to her daughter, is available. Here, the sentimentality noted by Murphy remains a primary characteristic, but the political and social protest has undergone a change. While the protest is still in the background, the foreground is a plea for the regeneration of the human soul. Furthermore, one sees no evidence of the attack on capitalism that Murphy reported. Rather, Todd proposes an amorphous spiritual regeneration to eliminate the personal greed bred by a competitive system. By competitive system she means the competition between employer and employee over the distribution of profits rather than the competition between one business firm and another. She does not attack private ownership of the means of production; instead, she views it as the instrument "to help change conditions for the betterment of God's children."[12]

The plot of this novel revolves around well-born Claudia and her search for a husband among three suitors. Her father wants her to marry Paul Clayton, a successful business man, but Claudia refuses; she cannot "love at will." She prefers the new minister, Phillip Vance, who, though motherless at age ten, "possessed (his mother's) great heart, broad intelligence, and intuitive sense."[13] Phillip appears at first to reciprocate Claudia's affection, but after a long discourse with his close friend, Henry Arthur, Phillip discovers that he doesn't love Claudia. Henry persuades Phillip the marriage would be a mistake. When Claudia learns of his change of heart, she swoons, sickens, almost dies. Conveniently widowed, conveniently wealthy, "generous and kind, frank and fearless," Henry himself woos and wins Claudia.[14]

The book has little action and much talk--talk about evolution, growth, reincarnation, and the burdens of the rich. This conversation seems shallow and unrealistic to twentieth-century readers. Poverty is portrayed by a barefoot ten-year-old, Jack Thomas, and his dying friend, Dick. Though Jack is poorly educated and lives a rough, tough life, he has a sense of fair play and a deep love for his friend. Claudia meets Jack as he makes his way, orange-in-hand, to Dick's "dilapidated little cottage in the hollow." After Dick dies and is properly buried "in a pretty casket," thanks to Claudia, Claudia rewards Jack for being such a loving friend. Claudia, too, is rewarded for her generosity, not only by feeling properly virtuous but also by a life which will evolve happily onward and upward.

This form of justice, this repayment for helping those in need, also rewards Henry Arthur, the wealthy businessman who finally marries Claudia. He draws up a plan by which he will share his business profits with his workers. Unlike Henry's first wife, Claudia is sympathetic to his compassion for the poor and his sense of human justice. Their marriage will be a healthy one, "wholesome and beautiful," enlarging "the soul of humanity."[15]

Todd had promised in the introduction to her first novel that she would rouse her readers to the harsh realities of the world as the Populists saw it. While that promise is fulfilled in her political tracts, the sentimentality and simplistic answers in her novels make then less successful. In the final analysis, it is Marion Marsh Todd's total life work--as a politician, lecturer, and writer--that should be remembered as representative of the Populists' idealism and concern for common people.

NOTES

[1]Marion Marsh Todd, Protective Tariff Delusions, 1886, p. 101.

[2]Delusions, p. 49.

[3]Todd, Railways of Europe and America, 1893, p. 13.

[4]Railways, p. 3.

[5]Goldwin Smith, "Woman's Place in the State." The Forum, January, 1890, p. 519-520.

[6]Smith, p. 530.

[7]Professor Goldwin Smith and His Satellites in Congress, 1890, p. 151.

[8]Professor, p. 165.

[9]Professor, p. 163.

[10]Todd, Rachel's Pitiful History, 1895, Introduction.

[11]James, Edward T., ed. Notable American Women, Vol. III. (Cambridge, Ma: Belknap Press, 1971), p. 471.

[12]Claudia, p. 130.

[13]Claudia, p. 2.

[14]Claudia, p. 40.

[15]Claudia, p. 132.

MARY MAYO (1845 – 1903)

MARY MAYO
LEADER OF RURAL WOMEN

Marilyn Culpepper

"I love everybody so much, so much. I have wanted to make life a little easier, a little more enjoyable. I have wanted to help people to be kinder, truer, sweeter. And there is so much to do."

From a letter written a few
weeks before her death.

Thousands of "her children," college presidents as well as street urchins, affectionately called her "Mother Mayo." Her picture adorned the walls of farm homes throughout Michigan. Jennie Buell, her biographer, wrote of her:

> Because she affected men and women in like manner, collectively as well as singly, she was able to exert a lasting influence upon certain wide movements of people, of farm people most of all. In some instances, she initiated those movements or 'mothered' them to such a degree that their getting rooted in permanency is coupled inseparably with her name.[1]

Historians called her "one of the most remarkable women in Grange history."[2] The President of Massachusetts Agricultural College, later to become President of Michigan Agricultural College, said, "The story of her life is worth writing and reading, both because of what she did and for what she was."[3]

Her epithet for herself was "that little brown woman from the farm." What a misnomer! True, she was tanned from long hours of farm work, and granted, she was small in stature; however, her accomplishments on behalf of women, education, and the disadvantaged dwarfed those of many of her female, as well as her male, contemporaries.

Thanks to Mary Mayo's work in helping to educate and to persuade both college officials and legislators—as well as some chauvinistic farmers—a women's course (the home economics curriculum) and the first women's dormitory were established at Michigan Agricultural College, now Michigan State University.

Her efforts did not stop at higher education for women, however. Her work with the Michigan Grange, an organization dedicated to improving rural life, touched the lives of many. In the Grange, Mary Mayo helped to institute the "Fresh Air" program and served for fourteen years as a leader of the Women's Work Committee. She wrote inspiring bi-monthly columns for the Grange newspaper and delivered speeches for the Grange and Farmers' Institutes, which reached thousands of men and women throughout the state, igniting within them visions of what they could accomplish for themselves or in concert for a cause.

As a member of the Board of Control of the State Industrial Home for Girls, Mary Mayo "mothered" hundreds of unfortunate girls. By helping to secure good foster homes for these girls and by encouraging them to lead meaningful, productive lives, she succeeded in transforming a host of young girls, once lost to themselves and to society, into worthwhile human beings.

She was born Mary Anne Bryant on May 25, 1845, on a farm near Battle Creek, Michigan, her ancestors hardy English and early New England stock. For the Bryant family, education was the all-important basis for a happy, worthwhile existence, and it was this conviction which became a driving force throughout Mayo's life. As a young child, she studied reading and writing in a private school conducted by two maiden aunts. Following her graduation from the Battle Creek high school, she affirmed her commitment to education by becoming a teacher in a district school. Three years later, she gave up teaching to marry Perry Mayo, a Bryant neighbor and recently returned Civil War veteran. A survivor of wounds sustained at Knoxville and in the Battle of the Wilderness and greatly matured by his wartime experiences, Perry Mayo was himself a literate, compassionate young man, bent on a college education before the war intervened.

Together they must have struck a marvelous match, each imbued with a deep commitment to farming, to education, and to their fellow human beings. Yet their married life was not an easy one. Farming, particularly in those days, entailed an exhausting routine of house and field work. In addition to her household chores, Mayo had to look after the chickens and grow the vegetables. Yet she was never too proud or too tired to lend a hand in the fields. The first Mayo home was a log cabin adjacent to the Bryant homestead, and the young couple put in long hours to make a success of their farm.

A chance encounter with a former classmate in a Battle Creek store helped to provide direction for Mary Mayo's future life. In recalling the incident, she explained how the acquaintance had patronizingly remarked that "as I had married a farmer, about all I had to do, or did do, was to work hard and make lots of good butter. While riding home with Mr. Mayo, I kept thinking it over. I knew that I did work hard and that I made good butter, but it made me indignant to think that this was the measure of my life and that of every farmer's wife. We both decided we would do something."[4] That "something" was to become a lifetime commitment to the work and perpetuation of the Grange.

Originating in 1867 in Washington, D.C. and dedicated to the education and advancement of farmers, the Grange, officially known as the Order of the Patrons of Husbandry, promised great political and social potential for the American farmer. The Grange, it was believed, could provide a concerted influence on education, local and national politics, economics, and social welfare. For women, who were admitted from the organization's inception as equals with men, Grange participation offered socially approved outlets for their mental and physical energies and a companionship and sisterhood which became the salvation of many isolated farm women.

Today's woman may have difficulties understanding the Grange movement, until she contemplates life on a farm in the latter quarter of the nineteenth century--life without telephones, cars, television sets, or any of the hundreds of conveniences so familiar to contemporary life. Housework and farm chores allowed little time for relaxation, reading, or socializing. Grange meetings, however, offered a hiatus from routine and an opportunity to meet, study, and work with others, or to join in projects to improve the lives of women and their families.[5] Grange activities provided an outlet for creativity and self expression, a sort of "rural arm of the women's rights movement." Since it was assumed that the lectures and meetings would result in better meals and more attractive homes, Grange activities were sanctioned by even the most skeptical husbands.[6] For lonely farm women, such as the mother of fourteen who hadn't seen anyone outside of her immediate family for five years, the Grange must have been heavensent.[7] In Mayo's eyes, "the Grange was to the farm women what the club was to the city woman and more...."[8]

The Mayos' early work was with neighborhood groups and the Farmers' Club, but when a local Grange was formed in their area in the 1870's, both of them channeled their time and efforts into the growing organization. Their peers, sensing their seemingly boundless energies and abilities, quickly elevated the Mayos from the county level to important state Grange offices. Although they often worked together in the perpetuation of Grange activities, in time their special interests and talents led them along different pathways. Perry Mayo became a Grange lecturer, an "Overseer," and an active member of numerous Grange committees. He also served as a state senator from 1887-88 and was a candidate for lieutenant governor in 1890. His wife's innovative ideas and unswerving energy found their mark primarily in women's activities, where she soon became recognized as "the leader of Michigan's rural women."[9]

Even in her early Grange activities, Mayo earned an enviable reputation for efficiency and hard work, and when her peers witnessed her ability to attract and captivate audiences, she was inundated with requests to speak throughout the state. Women speakers were not commonplace for farm audiences, or even city audiences, in the late nineteenth century, and on the occasion of her first trip outside her own county, a nervous Mayo was convinced that many people came "just out of curiosity to hear a woman speak. Some ridiculed," she reported, "a few were indignant."[10] Other listeners, however, were mesmerized by her sincerity and her plain good sense. In fact, so charmed were many of them that they begged her to stay to speak to the school children the next day. Thus began a speaking career which was to encompass hundreds of lectures for the Grange and later for the Farmers' Institutes. It was in this role as lecturer that

Mayo was able to bring to the people of Michigan her threefold message of sisterhood, of the vital importance of education for women, and of a Christian's fundamental commitment to charity.

Her speeches, we are told, were characterized by a certain eloquence—a straight-forward, direct approach which had a special appeal for her listeners. She spoke as one of them, in metaphors of the wheat field, the seasons, the harvest—analogies which made her talks seem less like sermons or admonitions and more like motherly advice and concern. Her Biblical and literary allusions were familiar phrases to her audiences; her everyday examples were references they could understand. Even the most mundane secretary's report for the local Grange took on a certain style when penned by Mary Mayo. As she spoke, usually without notes, young and old discovered a friend, a woman who was one of them, someone who had experienced their trials and failures. Yet it seemed to be her optimism, the promise of what each listener could achieve for herself or for her family, which so enraptured her audiences. The subtle persuasion and words of encouragement uplifted the most distressed spirits and left her listeners refreshed and inspired.

In part, it was through these speeches that Mayo achieved her most far-reaching success—the development of a women's course and the building of a women's dormitory on the Michigan Agricultural College campus. For years, her dreams had been not only the admission of women to Michigan Agricultural College, but also the creation of a special course for women and the building of a dormitory to properly house these new enrollees.

Although women had been admitted to the College in 1870, their numbers were limited to those who could find housing in neighboring homes. A further deterrent was the curriculum: agricultural courses in plowing, crop fertilization, maintenance of farm equipment, and dairy hygiene. These courses, Mayo contended, were not appropriate for farm girls and certainly not for city girls. They needed a curriculum of their own, designed to increase their knowledge and efficiency as future homemakers, the role relegated to most women at that time. "Parents today," Mayo wrote, "are anxious that their daughters shall be as thoroughly trained for the practical work of their lives as are their sons."[11] Thus the development of courses in domestic science and art at Michigan Agricultural College became a favored topic for Mayo as she toured the state on numerous speaking engagements. She also prodded state Grange officials into repeatedly supporting a resolution advocating courses for women at the college.

Now, of course, if the women's course were to be successful, a women's dormitory would be mandatory. Finally, in 1896 the college officials, after considerable education and persuasion, transferred a group of male students to other dorms and rooms in nearby homes, and Abbot Hall was converted into the domestic economy building. By renovating the dormitory and adding a sewing room and cooking laboratory, the college was able to accommodate forty women students. Mayo's ideas were validated, for the new course quickly proved so popular that construction of a larger building became necessary. In 1900 the Women's Building was completed and immediately dubbed the "Coop" by the male student body. The new building housed 120 young women, laboratories, music rooms, and a gymnasium.[12] Mary Mayo's dream had at last become a reality! At the dedication, some 500 women gave her a standing ovation. Only the illness of her daughter prevented her from sharing in the celebration.

Mary Mayo also worked long and hard in continuing education for farm women. As Farmers' Institutes grew in popularity, Kenyon L. Butterfield, later president of Michigan Agricultural College, decided to hold special sections for women. The Farmers' Institutes were short courses offered under the auspices of the college and conducted in various localities throughout the state by local sponsoring groups. The Institutes drew heavily upon Grange memberships for both speakers and audiences. To introduce and develop his idea for women, Butterfield sought Mary Mayo's help. "My heart just throbbed," she later recalled. "It was what I had long wanted to do." She later wrote to Butterfield, "There are hosts of topics that need bringing to the 'wimin.' While we gladly listen to papers upon the scientific feeding of farm stock, we want to know something about the scientific feeding of the human animal. We can understand something of the relative value of a silo and the best way to construct a barn; but we want also to know how best to build the home so that its influence upon each member of the family may be most helpful."[13]

The Farmers' Institutes held tremendous appeal for Mayo. She was convinced that women were eager to spend their time more profitably than in merely sipping tea and socializing. On November 14, 1895, however, as the first meeting of the "Women's Sections" convened, even the ever-confident Mayo was fearful about their reception. Allotted a small reading room and a few chairs for the meeting, Mayo opened the session by speaking for about 30 minutes about the problems facing farm women and the need for study and further education. Following her speech, she sat down discouraged, convinced that her idea had been a failure. Happily, her fears were unwarranted, for with her enthusiasm and organizing skill, the women's sections became immediately successful. That year and in the years which followed, women flocked to the meetings. Some 5,309 women were estimated to have attended Mayo's twenty institutes and the state meeting held in 1895. The next year, 1896-97, found her participating in forty-five institutes; in 1897-98 there were twenty-eight; in

1898-99 she participated in eighteen; in 1899-1900 she participated in twelve.[14]

Such topics as nutrition, cooking, homemaking, and child care were early subjects for institute speakers, but with Mary's prompting, speakers soon ventured into more challenging territory with such issues as "Heredity and Maternity," "The Farmers' Daughters--Where Shall They be Educated?" "How Much of the Profits of the Farm Should the Wife Receive During the Life of Her Husband and How Much at his Death?"[15]

Mayo not only organized and conducted many of the women's sections and served as one of the most sought-after speakers, but also took an active role in securing and training other institute speakers. She bolstered the timid and hesitant with her optimistic "Yes, you can; I know you can." Over the years, many an inexperienced farm wife, sustained by Mayo's engaging spirit and assurance, became a successful lecturer. Mayo would herself take the most difficult topics and the most exhausting trips in order to encourage the novice to persevere. Small wonder her listeners felt that "the other women helped us and we liked them, but we loved Mrs. Mayo."[16]

Education was merely one facet of Mary Mayo's accomplishments. As chairman of the Woman's Work committee of the Michigan Grange, Mary Mayo encouraged the local Granges in organizing fund raisers to pay off Grange meeting hall mortgages, purchase new furnishings and equipment, and extend the organization's charitable work to hospitals and the underprivileged. One of her most significant contributions, however, was her plan for sending indigent, sickly city children, tired working girls, and exhausted mothers with young babies to farm homes for two weeks of healthy, country living. Host farm families were encouraged to invite a child or a mother and baby into their homes during the summer months when the days were suffocating and miserable in the city and when food was plentiful on the farms.

In 1893 when the project was introduced, it was met with mass confusion. City dwellers wondered why farmers would be willing to accept perfect strangers into their homes for a two-week free vacation. In turn, farm women questioned whether already overworked farm wives could take on one more mouth to feed, one more child to care for. Everyone wanted to know who would pay the transportation costs. Who would select the children? Would the children get homesick? In a matter of months, Mayo and her committee had engaged the help of social service directors and YWCA secretaries, selected needy children, and successfully persuaded farm wives that, despite extra work, there would be untold rewards in satisfaction and good feelings for their efforts. Railroad companies were induced to provide reduced fares for the travellers; some companies even volunteered free transportation. Buoyed by Mayo's enthusiasm, the project quickly took hold, fears were allayed, host families secured, and in 1894 more than one hundred children were treated to a taste of country life and down-home hospitality. "Mother Mayo," of course, took the lead by inviting two girls into her home, one with an advanced case of consumption. By the end of the summer, the response on both sides was so positive that the following year 189 more people enjoyed carefree summer vacations in the country. As word spread, the popularity of the project escalated and it became a yearly event. The <u>Detroit Free Press</u> provided publicity and instituted a Fresh Air Fund which it initiated with a $25.00 contribution. Contrary to some Grangers' fears, the whole project was conducted at absolutely no expense to the Grange, other than a few dollars for postage and stationery.[17] Part of Mayo's job was to place children with compatible families. She also found permanent homes with farm families for a great many young orphans. Testimonials to the success of the outings permeated her reports at the State Grange Annual Meetings and her columns for The Grange Visitor. One of the most poignant accounts was about one small boy who, with pockets bulging with peaches for the trip back to the city, hugged his host family and exclaimed, "Now I guess I know what Heaven is like!"[18]

Mayo's work for the Grange also included the inauguration of Children's Days. With the growth of the cities and the wealth of opportunities in business and management, farm life was becoming less and less attractive for many young people. Mayo was convinced that farming would take on greater appeal if children were to become interested in agricultural pursuits at a young age. With this bonding to the rural life in mind, Mayo helped to introduce Children's Days, Grange meetings planned especially for children, with youngsters reading essays, giving recitations, composing poetry, and presenting the entire programs themselves. The meetings, initiated in June of 1886, were followed by special feasts where the children were treated as honored guests.[19] The idea met with considerable enthusiasm, and soon Children's Days became annual events not only in Michigan Granges, but in Granges across the country.

In her bi-monthly columns beginning in 1886 for the Michigan Grange newspaper, The Grange Visitor, Mayo succeeded in touching the lives of still more Michigan farmers. Each column focused on a topic selected to provoke discussion among women and most were on practical subjects, such as proper ventilation, the efficient disposal of kitchen wastes, the rewards of a cheerful disposition, and the need to share books and magazines.

In a column in July 1886, she agreed with physicians that "corsets were the cause of more than two-thirds the ills that women are heir to...." and urged women to discontinue wearing them. In another column, she instructed her readers not to fill their cellars with apple juice that would ferment into hard cider. Later on, she suggested that women devote far less precious time to preparing pies and other delicacies. That time, she wrote, could be better spent in self-improvement and reading.

Cognizant of Mayo's work on behalf of the poor and oppressed, Cyrus G. Luce, former Master of the Michigan Grange, appointed her to the Board of Control of the State Industrial Home for Girls when he became governor of Michigan in 1887. Here Mayo met one of her most severe challenges: the placement of girls on probation or released from the home into good foster homes. The job required skill--placement of the right girls with the right families; patience--relocation of girls who were incorrigible or who could not adapt to their new surroundings; and perseverance--conviction that these girls could be helped to discover a better life. All three qualities Mayo possessed in abundance. Her work helped many young women to turn their lives around, transcend their past mistakes, and embark on successful, worthwhile lives. In chapel talks at the State Home, Mayo rallied the residents to a more healthy respect for themselves and society. In her work with the matrons and officers, she roused them to a new confidence and enthusiasm for their often discouraging tasks. In her work with the girls personally, she became their confidante, their "Mother Mayo."

Mary Mayo's life was grounded in Christianity. Although she served in many Grange offices, one of her longest-held positions was that of State Grange Chaplain, a role normally assigned to a member of the clergy. Her guidepost throughout her life work, was the Christian message: "Love thy neighbor." For Mayo this meant loving her family, her friends, even strangers--a daily commitment to others extending to even the smallest of gestures. Her religion was the Christian spirit manifested in a warm smile for a harassed grocery clerk, a hearty dinner for an ailing neighbor, or a hamper of food for weary travellers. She found her happiness in doing for others in the practical, everyday business of life. For Mayo the opportunity to lighten a neighbor's load, to lift up a discouraged soul, to help foster a reconciliation, constituted not only the duty of life, but the very essence of life itself. Hers was no "Sunday only" Christianity, but rather a genuine, omnipresent love of humanity.

Her consistent theme was the sanctity of the family circle and the vital need for communication among family members. She exhorted people everywhere to cherish familial relationships, to treasure each day and to make the most of it, to take time to enjoy all of life's blessings.

What she counselled for others, Mary Mayo practiced in her own life. Despite her unceasing work for the Grange, Mary's first concerns were always for her family. Her children's education and her family's comfort and happiness were top priorities. When her daughter Nellie was invalided as the result of an accident, Mayo stayed at her bedside constantly and ceased her vigil only three weeks before her own death on April 21, 1903.

It was not until 1931 that a new women's dormitory at Michigan State University was named in her honor. The dedication for "that little brown woman from the farm" who devoted her life to mothering people and causes was long overdue.

NOTES

[1] Jennie Buell, One Woman's Work for Farm Women (Boston: Jennie Buell, 1908), p. 3.

[2] Fred Trump, The Grange in Michigan: An Agricultural

History of Michigan Over the Past Ninety Years (Grand Rapids, Mich.: Fred Trump, 1963), p. 32.

[3] Buell, p. vi.

[4] Buell, p. 9.

[5] Donald B. Marti, "Woman's Work in the Grange: Mary Ann Mayo of Michigan, 1882-1903," Agricultural History, April 1982, p. 440.

[6] Donald B. Marti, "Sisters of the Grange: Rural Feminism in the Late Nineteenth Century," Agricultural History, July 1984, p. 252.

[7] Buell, p. 20.

[8] Buell, p. 32.

[9] Madison Kuhn, Michigan State: The First Hundred Years (East Lansing: Michigan State University Press, 1955), p. 240.

[10] Buell, p. 23.

[11] Kuhn, p. 220.

[12] Maude Gilchrist, The First Three Decades of Home Economics at Michigan State College (East Lansing: School of Home Economics, 1947), pp. 1-17.

[13] Buell, p. 53.

[14] Buell, p. 56.

[15] Buell, p. 54

[16] Buell, p. 65.

[17] Michigan State Grange Proceedings 1894 (Lansing: Robert Smith & Co., 1894), p. 441.

[18] Mary Mayo, "Outings for Working Girls and Children from the City," The Grange Visitor, Vol. 19, May 3, 1894, p. 3.

[19] Trump, p. 34.

ANNA HOWARD SHAW (1847 – 1919)

ANNA HOWARD SHAW
ORATOR

Dorothy and Lawrence Giel

Anna Howard Shaw was born in Newcastle-on-Tyne, England, on February 14, 1847. In 1851, when she was four, she moved to the United States with her family. They lived first in New Bedford and Lawrence, Massachusetts, and then moved to an isolated pioneer farm near Big Rapids, Michigan.

According to her autobiography, Shaw supplemented the early education she had received in Massachusetts with omnivorous reading of her own, and at fifteen she became a teacher in a frontier school.[1] Following the Civil War, she moved to the home of a married sister in Big Rapids and attended the local high school. She became active in the Methodist church, preached her first sermon at Ashton, Michigan, in 1870, and was licensed (not ordained) to preach in 1871. A stone monument has since been erected in Ashton, marking the site where Shaw delivered her first sermon.

Deciding to prepare for the ministry, she enrolled in 1873 at Albion College, where she worked her way through two years of study. In 1876 she entered the theological school at Boston University, from which she graduated in 1878, after two years of nearly desperate poverty. Shaw was the second woman ever to enter the theological school and the only woman to graduate in her particular class.

She became pastor of the Methodist Episcopal Church at Hingham, Massachusetts, in 1878, and also served the parish at East Dennis from 1878 to 1886. She was refused ordination by the New England Conference of the Methodist Episcopal Church because of her sex but was invested by the Protestant Methodist Church in 1880, the first woman ever ordained by that denomination. While ministering to her Cape Cod parishes, Shaw managed to earn a medical degree from Boston University in 1886, a rare occurrence for women at that time. Shaw never married but adopted Howard as a middle name when she entered public life, probably because the name suggested widowhood, a more socially acceptable state than spinsterhood for women in the nineteenth century.

Shaw's ministerial duties and medical background made her acutely aware of the myriad problems and inequities that existed in society. She was national superintendent of franchise for the Women's Christian Temperance Union from 1886-1892. In 1886, she resigned her pastorates and became a lecturer for the Massachusetts Woman Suffrage Association. A meeting with Susan B. Anthony in 1888 introduced her to the work of the National American Woman Suffrage Association (NAWSA). In 1891 she became national lecturer for the NAWSA, and from 1892 to 1904 she was vice-president of the organization. During those years, she traveled and lectured and was accounted as the most eloquent and moving orator in the suffrage cause. She succeeded Carrie Chapman Catt to the presidency of the NAWSA in 1904 and held the post until 1915, when she received the title of honorary president.

In her autobiography, Shaw relates how Susan B. Anthony persuaded her to drop temperance work and concentrate on the suffrage cause. Anthony was herself a prohibitionist who nevertheless believed that the cause of woman suffrage could not win without the vote of many anti-prohibitionists. Most temperance men would vote for woman suffrage in any case, but Anthony concluded that "the wets" could hardly be induced to vote favorably after being told that the beneficiaries of their decision would promptly deprive them of their glass of wine. She convinced Shaw that these men were not to be made so angry that they would vote against equal suffrage. Besides, "you can't win two causes at once," Anthony reminded Shaw. "You're merely scattering your energies."[2]

The decision was difficult for Shaw as she believed that alcohol abuse was a major social problem causing untold misery within the family and the workplace. "But Miss Anthony's arguments were irrefutable, and she was herself, as always, irresistible."[3]

During World War I, President Woodrow Wilson asked Anna Shaw to form and chair the Women's Committee of the United States Council of National Defense. For her outstanding wartime effort in this capacity, she became the second woman recipient of the Distinguished Service Medal in 1919. After the armistice in 1918, former President William Taft and President A. Lawrence Lowell of Harvard University prevailed upon her to exercise her considerable oratorical skills to promote Wilson's ill-fated League of Nations.

Throughout her illustrious career, Shaw's primary sources of financial support were the speaking engagements frequently arranged through the Redpath Speaking Bureau. In her lifetime, it is estimated that she delivered as many as 10,000 speeches, mostly on the topic of woman suffrage. She spoke in every state of the Union and was the first ordained woman to preach at the universities of Amsterdam, Berlin, Christiana, Copenhagen, and London. Many considered her to be the finest female orator of her day.[4]

Dr. Anna Howard Shaw died at her home in Moylan, Pennsylvania, on July 2, 1919, living long enough to see a favorable vote on the 19th Amendment by Congress but not its ratification by the states in 1920.

Shaw spent her life in devotion to causes. Each cause was larger in scope than the previous one. She went from country school teaching to ministry, to advocating prohibition, to supporting women's suffrage, and finally to advocating a plan for world peace. She was an idealist who believed she had a purpose in life: to improve the world. In October, 1983, Shaw was honored posthumously as one of the first honorees of the Michigan Woman's Hall of Fame.

Although Dr. Shaw spoke for the Women's Temperance Society early in her career and in her final years campaigned for the United States to enter the League of Nations, her most famous oratorical efforts were aimed at the passage of a constitutional amendment giving women the right to vote.

Dr. Shaw did not follow the lead of her fellow suffragist, Alice Paul, who patterned her strategy after the English suffragists with dramatic demonstrations and picketing to advance the cause. Like Carrie Chapman Catt, Shaw preferred gradual education and persuasion.[5]

She did not become associated with any political party. To do so would have compromised her principles. Shaw claimed, "I have too much respect for myself to align myself with any party until my vote is valuable enough to be counted in the ballot box. We don't appeal to the men of any party, but to the manhood of American men."[6]

Her autobiography, The Story of a Pioneer, is written in an interesting conversational style. The inverted sentence structure and flowery words and phrases one often sees in books of the period are missing and the sentence structure is straight-forward with subjects preceding verbs and modifiers sensibly placed. She rarely uses obscure terminology, but picturesque and eloquent language abounds. Such phrases as "arctic loneliness," "expenses outran my income," and "Heaven held no lamps aloft to guide us and soon darkness folded around us like a garmet," add vitality and verve to her writing and conjure up vivid mental pictures.[7] She avoided cliches, relying instead on a quick wit and ready imagination to convey her message.

All referrals to herself are related with utmost modesty as if she were unaware of her vital role in history. The autobiography is replete with stories of pioneer days in west-central Michigan, the social, economic, and political obstacles placed in the path of women, and the joys and frustrations of fighting for feminine rights. Shaw writes revealing tales of Susan B. Anthony, Elizabeth Cady Stanton, Stephen Foster, Ralph Waldo Emerson, and Carrie Chapman Catt, as well as stories of lumbermen, sailors, and homemakers—in brief, a cross-section of American life at that time.

Shaw's suffrage speeches were delivered to a variety of audiences. Her wide-spread reputation as an outstanding orator was earned on the campaign circuit as she plugged for women's rights. As in all oratory, Shaw's words need to be read aloud to fully appreciate her oratorical skills. The reader is advised to do so in the following examples. Shaw always appealed to reason in her argument for woman suffrage. She contended that the U.S. Constitution provided for a representative form of government. Women were not being represented because they lacked the vote; therefore, there could be no true representative government until women were given the vote. The same deductive logic is found in virtually all of Shaw's speeches. If she were alive today, Shaw's arguments in support of the Equal Rights Amendment would probably use the same deductive logic.

In a strikingly contemporary argument, she demonstrates that woman's suffrage is necessary to preserve the home.

Every woman must have a home before she can do anything there. A house is not a home. A woman may be a very excellent housekeeper but a very poor home maker. She may be a very estimable home maker but a very poor housekeeper. The terms home and house are not by any means synonymous. It may be possible that in order to make a home a woman must leave her house a great deal. It may be quite possible that a woman may do as much outside of her house for her home as she does inside for her home.[8]

Shaw branded prejudice and tradition as the two greatest enemies of the suffrage movement.[9] Thus breaking down traditional barriers and refuting prejudicial charges were major objectives in her campaign. Dr. Shaw answered the charge that women were attempting to enter men's rightful sphere of operation as follows:

Is it not marvelous that woman would go out of her sphere? I have been out of it for about twenty-two years, and I think have been about as comfortable as most women who have been in it. How difficult it is for man to get out of his sphere. Did you ever know of a man getting out of his sphere? I never did in all my life. I used to wonder how it was that woman could get out of her sphere so easily and it was so difficult for a man to get out of his sphere, until I discovered that man hadn't any sphere. I have noticed this, however, that if man doesn't get out of his sphere, he gets into ours. I saw men waiters at the tables. Men served the food, and I have no doubt that men cooked it. Three-fourths of the women were created for the very purpose of cooking. Now, a man has entered that sphere. When I was a girl they paid a dollar and a half a week to a girl for this work. Now, they pay from one thousand to ten thousand dollars a year for a cook, and the cook is a man. When the salary is this latter sum, then it is man's sphere; but when the low wages are paid, then it is a woman's sphere.[10]

Note the clever manner in which Shaw turns the tables on the male argument. While women operate in a limited sphere, the male is limited only by those undesirable female spheres which they prefer not to enter.

In 1960, Wilmer W. Linkugel collected, classified, and edited Shaw's speeches, working with archival material deposited at Radcliffe College. Linkugel describes the physical characteristics and rhetorical style of Shaw as follows:

> Thus we can picture Dr. Shaw, the suffrage orator, as an energetic, short and stout woman with beautiful white hair combed back and twisted over the crown of her head. Underneath her broad brows dark eyes sparkled expressively as she spoke. She had great dignity and stood solidly on the platform in a cool and somewhat lofty manner. As she came forward with a smile to greet her audience, hands folded in front of her, she radiated motherly love and sincerity, thereby disarming the prejudice of most listeners. She began to speak in a rich contralto voice, which was clear and distinct, in no way raucous--sometimes even quiet, but so well projected that it could be heard in the largest halls. Words flowed easily and fluently and were enforced by frequent gestures and considerable facial expression. It was difficult to evade her spell. The listener soon realized that this was a well educated woman with a well trained mind. Her doctor's degrees added to her dignity.[11]

Photographs of Dr. Shaw reveal that she was attired in dark, conservative dresses for most speaking engagements. On ceremonial occasions she would sometimes don academic regalia. The following excerpts taken from Linkugel dissertation show how relevant Shaw's ideas are for modern day feminists. Listen to the voice of Shaw on higher education for women:

> We (women) knocked at the doors of our colleges. The doors were beaten down; our young women went in. They said, if you come in we will have to lower the grade of scholarship to the intellectual capabilities of women. But they did not lower the grade. And today Miss Fawcett stands 600 points above the senior wrangler in mathematics in England, and Miss Brown takes the prize in classics from the foremost students at Harvard, through the Annex (Radcliffe). It was discovered that we have brains which when cultivated would turn out as good work as the brains of men.[12]

Shaw related how at one time she wanted to enter the male-dominated Boston police force as an officer. When asked if she could knock a man down and take him to jail she replied:

> My idea is not so much to arrest criminals as it is to prevent crime. When I lived for three years in the back alleys of Boston, I saw there what was needed to prevent crime and from that day to this I believe that there is no great public gathering of any sort whatever where we do not need women on the police force; ....and we will have them there some day.[13]

In each of the above excerpts, the modern feminist theme of male and female equality is evident. Anna Howard Shaw paved the way for late twentieth century changes in employment and education.

Any discussion of this great orator would be incomplete without examining her clever use of wit and irony. Here are selected examples:

> It has been argued that women were inferior to men because their brains weigh less. The quantity not the quality of brains is taken into consideration in this estimate. A man in the slums of Boston who killed himself by drinking seventeen glasses of beer on a wager was found to have a larger brain then Daniel Webster.

> The Scriptures, some say, teach that the man is the head of the family; but if that is so, the head in a great many cases gets on the wrong body.[14]

> There is a clergyman in the South. He will not allow a woman to talk in the church or to teach in the Sunday School because she makes a loud noise. He would not even allow her to teach in the infant class if there was a male infant in the class. I have the profoundest respect for that man. He is an idiot, but consistent.[15]

Shaw frequently asked her audiences to place questions in a box from which she would draw at the end of her lecture, responding extemporaneously. Shaw's audience looked forward to this part of the presentation because of the witty answers they had learned to expect. For example:

> Q: If women had the ballot, would she not sell her vote for a new bonnet?
> Shaw: Perhaps she might. Who knows: A new bonnet is a fine thing, and most women hanker after it. But a good bonnet costs more than a glass of whiskey, and that, they say, is the market price of male votes nowadays.
> Q: Why does the Scripture say that there shall be no marriages in heaven?
> Shaw: Ah, my dear friends (and she drew a long sigh), someone has answered that by saying, because there will be no men there.[16]

In his extensive research, Linkugel found that even those who disagreed with Shaw generally didn't take offense and seemed instead to enjoy her clever wit and quick, incisive retorts.[17]

Shaw generally attempted to allay hostility by depersonalizing her message. She rarely named names and her narrative usually involved people placed in other localities. For example, stories told in western states usually involved "someone" from New York or New Jersey. By using different localities as the settings for her preachments, she allowed the audience to laugh at the foibles of other people and not feel personally ridiculed or lampooned. Shaw also cushioned her barbs by attributing them to depersonalized others. Her responses to questions were replete with "they say" or "someone has said." Undoubtedly these rhetorical devices aided in making her oratory less personally offensive.

Perhaps another important factor in Shaw's humor being accepted by a relatively hostile audience was the image she portrayed, particularly in her later years. It was hard to take offense at a white haired, chubby, mother-figure with a friendly smile and dancing eyes.

In Carry Chapman Catt's eulogy for Dr. Anna Howard Shaw she said, "with her cutting ridicule and biting sarcasm she could cut intolerance wide open until its fallacies lay bare for all to see. But as the cause gained she put aside this ridicule and sarcasm and assumed a gentler and sunnier humor."[18]

Perhaps Catt's statement is accurate. Perhaps not. Certainly Shaw's thirty years of campaign speeches on suffrage, as collected by Wilmar Linkugel, do not clearly reflect this change. Maybe the pronouncements which sounded like ridicule when spoken by the young Shaw were perceived as "sunny humor" when delivered by an older, more matronly orator.

Anna Howard Shaw was an ardent feminist and an idealist in the best sense of the term. She started out to improve individual morality by becoming a minister, tried to improve society by moving into the temperance and suffrage movements, and finally campaigned vigorously for an organization to promote world peace. Each cause she pursued was larger in scope than the preceding. Anna Howard Shaw's great strength lay in her peerless ability as an orator to voice the demands of moral reform and to challenge the conscience of the nation. For her entire career, she strove to convince the American public to live up to their ideals.

NOTES

[1]Shaw, Anna Howard, The Story of a Pioneer, New York: Harper Brothers Publishers),1915. Biographical details throughout the essay are taken from this source.

[2]Shaw, p. 182.

[3]Shaw, p. 182.

[4]Linkugel, Wilmer W., The Speeches of Anna Howard Shaw: Collected and Edited with Introduction and Notes, (Madison: University of Wisconsin, doctoral dissertation), 1960.

[5]Jordan et al, The United States, 5th edition, (New Jersey: Prentice-Hall, Inc.), 1982, p. 568.

[6]Shaw in Linkugel, p. 142.

[7]Shaw, The Story of a Pioneer, p. 77.

[8]Shaw in Linkugel, p. 103.

[9]Linkugel, p. 90.

[10]Shaw in Linkugel, p. 93.

[11]Linkugel, p. 167.

[12]Shaw in Linkugel, p. 95.

[13]Shaw in Linkugel, p. 286.

[14]Shaw in Linkugel, p. 114.

[15]Shaw in Linkugel, p. 91.

[16]Shaw in Linkugel, p. 194.

[17]Linkugel, p. 193.

[18]Harper, Ida Husted, History of Woman Suffrage, Vol. 5, (New York: Arno Press), 1969, p. 612.

ELLA WING MERRIMAN SHARP (1857 - 1912)

ELLA WING MERRIMAN SHARP
CONSERVATIONIST

Lynnea Loftis and Natalie Field

When Ella Wing Merriman Sharp was born on Hillside Farm near Jackson, Michigan, the area was growing rapidly. The early pioneer period when trees were regarded as enemies, to be eliminated as fast as possible, had passed. Although her New York grandfather, Abraham Wing, had made a part of his fortune in lumber, his granddaughter would one day be recognized as a public benefactor precisely for helping to preserve Michigan's forests. Wing had purchased land in Michigan as an investment. His daughter Mary and her new husband, Dwight Merriman, settled down there to take advantage of the young state's fast growing economy and to develop a "magnificent farm."[1] Their first children, Ella and her twin brother Frank, were born in 1857.

1859 was a difficult year for the family. Dwight Merriman was in ill health and Frankie was a frail child. With a new son, Tracy, to care for also, Mary Merriman had more than she could handle and little "Ellie" was taken to New York to spend several months with her grandparents. During this visit Abraham Wing wrote, "She now says everything and talks all the time and it takes one of the girls all the time to follow her as she is running from one room to another."[2] When Frankie, died of a childhood disease at the age of four, little Ella took exclusive possession of the position of eldest child. Another brother, Howard, was born in 1863.

She grew up in an environment that encouraged her to appreciate the natural world around her and to share these blessings with others. She was also blessed with the financial resources to enable her to do so. And those resources were hers! Hillside Farm passed to her from her grandfather's estate. Though she did not build her fortune from nothing, it came from her side of the family and she did not have to consider a husband's wishes in disposing of it.

The Victorian Period was one of great interest in nature and of belief in nature's healing, beneficial influence. Even indoors, reminders of nature were everywhere. Walls and floorcoverings were patterned with flowers. Some of the furniture at Hillside Farm had carved fruit or grain decoration or was inlaid with animal figures, and a wreath of seeds, leaves, and flowers was considered a suitable wall decoration. The girls' and women's magazines were full of directions for making household items using nature's materials or having a flower, leaf or animal motif. Her mother's interests included pressing leaves to preserve them and painting small studies of objects in nature. And of course her father, who was operating the farm, must have been well aware of the need to work with nature and not destroy resources that would be needed in future years.

In her mother, Ella Sharp had an example of a woman who worked together with other women to improve the lives of those who struggled with misfortune. Mary Merriman's girlhood education at Castleton Academy in Vermont had fostered her inclination to do this.

> "...the 1830's with the bonding together of women...in schools for women...produced women who had had the experience of friendship within a large society of females at a formative state in the development of their identity and they kept expecting it. They continued to

maintain patterns of working with other women throughout their adult lives..."[3]

Among other things, Mary Merriman was one of the chief organizers of the Home of the Friendless in Jackson. She was already familiar with the New York Home for the Friendless, having for many years made a practice of having a young girl from that home live at Hillsdale. The girl helped with the housework while the family was responsible for providing her with a home, food, clothing, and education. One such girl, Lulu Dart, later became a teacher of home economics at the fledgling Iowa State University. Such arrangements were important as it was very difficult for a woman without family resources to make her way in the world.

Though she began her formal education in the local schools, Sharp followed her mother's example and in 1872 went away to boarding school. After a brief period at a school in Ontario, she enrolled at the Michigan Female Seminary in Kalamazoo, which offered instruction in such subjects as Latin, higher mathematics, chemistry, ancient history, and English composition. According to the school's charter, its purpose was:

> "to establish endow, and control a Seminary of learning for the education of young ladies in the higher branches of a thorough education, having reference to the entire person, physically, intellectually, morally and religiously considered and to be essentially modeled after the Mt. Holyoke Seminary in Massachusetts, founded by Mary Lyon."[4]

Any father concerned that too much education might make his daughter forget that woman's place was in the home could be reassured by the statement in the school catalogue that pupils were expected to assist for one hour daily in the lighter domestic work as:

> "when there is complete isolation from the domestic department, a pupil goes out from school with a distaste for domestic duties which unfits her for a home life."[5]

Nonetheless, the "Fem Sem," as the girls liked to call it, put the impressionable young student in touch with women who believed that woman's place was more than just the home, and that she should be aware of the world around her. One such woman was Mary Cram Ellis, a young teacher who became a life long friend. The Ellis children were among the young people in whose development and education Sharp took an interest in later years.

Ella Merriman Sharp's attendance at the "Sem" was interrupted by a trip to Europe in 1873 with her mother. The trip appears to have been undertaken for Ella's health and Mrs. Merriman's letters home are often concerned with how well she is recovering and whether she is well enough to pursue the study of French.

Though Sharp resumed her formal education after her return, she does not appear to have graduated and in 1878 again took the opportunity to broaden her outlook and acquire new ideas in Europe. Not long after mother and daughter returned from this trip, Mary Merriman lost another son.

Though the experience of seeing yet another of her children die left her in a gloomy frame of mind, Merriman eventually recovered much of her animation and continued to write lively and interesting letters home from her various trips. She once wrote to her daughter from Paris, "went with Roie (a nephew) to see Pasteur give rabies treatments."[6]

With their frequent traveling and visiting, mother and daughter developed a wide network of friendly support which, like other Victorian women, they maintained through a steady exchange of letters. People they met on their travels, like Olive Sykes, an actress, and her husband Wirt, a free lance writer for the New York Times, or a Dr. and Mrs. Henderson who lived in England and "traveled", were added to their assortment of correspondents. They knew people who knew people. We don't know how she happened to be invited, but Merriman wrote on one occasion of "having tea at the White House with Mrs. Hayes" and during one of her many trips to Europe she accompanied her brother-in-law, an art dealer, as he toured the Vatican art collection.[7]

Ella Merriman Sharp's marriage to John C. Sharp in 1881 added a new dimension to her life and interests. Though the children she so eagerly awaited never came, she added to her understanding of how to make government serve the public needs through her husband's involvement in politics, particularly his term as a State Senator. Though John Sharp undoubtedly saw it as his responsibility to take care of many of his wife's business affairs, he made a point of consulting her before doing so. His professional correspondence of the 1870's and 1880's reflects his willingness to advise and represent women.

As the 25 year old Ella Sharp prepared "to go to housekeeping" in the spring of 1882, she was a busy young woman. In the next few years she would maintain an active correspondence with many relatives and friends, travel for social and health reasons, and become the mistress of Hillside Farm. In spite of some major health problems during this period, Sharp was very active and energetic and was sometimes cautioned by family and friends not to wear herself out "doing for others."[8]

It is difficult to say how Ella Sharp first became involved in women's groups, but during the 1880's women throughout the country were forming study clubs of all kinds. They wanted to be well informed and to have an opportunity to develop their cultural interests. In these clubs, women found not only interesting programs and stimulating discussion, but also new support groups. As the movement grew, these groups developed into a nation wide network. At the high point of membership, the women's club movement had some three million members in major urban centers around the United States.[9]

This was evidently a complex, interlocking system of communication. Ella Sharp, for example, belonged to at least two Jackson Women's Clubs--the Mosaic and the Athena. Both were founded in the middle 1880's as literary clubs. The fourteen Federated Women's Clubs in Jackson covered a wide range of interests. Some women wished to study literature, some history, and some music, art and current events. The programs of the state and national federations reflected this diversity. The fields chosen by the Federation of Women's Clubs for education and action involved forestry, parks and recreation, education, child labor and other types of child welfare, and civic improvement.

Education, particularly for girls, was a cause Ella Sharp supported for many years, both personally and through the Federation of Women's Clubs. As she had no children to raise, her impulses to guide and provide for the new generation took other paths. With the Michigan Female Seminary experiencing increased financial difficulties around the turn of the century, she worked hard to rally support for the school from its alumnae and various public benefactors. At the same time, she gave financial aid personally to some of the students. Her helpfulness to the young took other forms, from giving cookies to the passing school children, to presenting programs in the schools, to helping a young couple with building expenses.

Ella Sharp's individual involvement in the world around her grew along with the growth of the Women's Club movement. She was not a person to take a back seat. From leadership in her local clubs, she went on to assume responsibilities on the state level and became very active as a speaker at women's gatherings all over the state. The causes which the Women's Clubs took up were "in the air" at the time, but the clubs' programs focused women's energies and attention and gave them the information and backing to enable them to take confident stands and effective action. In the 1880's and 1890's, the idea was growing that cities could be unhealthy places and that open air and exercise were important remedies for some of society's ills. The works of popular writers like E.P. Roe and Will Carleton helped to spread this idea. A Carleton poem, "That Swamp of Death, A City Ballad," appeared on the front page of Harper's Weekly, September 17, 1881, and told of a poor father mourning the death of his young daughter who died, "choked and strangled by the foul breath of the chimneys over there."[10]

The periodicals of the day were of tremendous importance in forming public opinion. People clipped articles of particular interest to paste in scrapbooks or exchange with friends. It was quite common for Sharp, her mother, and their friends to send each other entire papers. Besides the local newspapers, the Merrimans and Sharps subscribed to many others including Harper's Weekly and Harper's Monthly, Moore's Rural New Yorker, Michigan Farmer, and Godey's Ladies Book. All of these, from time to time, depicted the ills of poverty and proposed solutions such as farm life and the open air as cures for everything from juvenile delinquency to tuberculosis.

Though Ella Sharp took a supportive interest in other items on the General Federation's agenda, the fields in which she became most actively involved were forestry and recreation and those aspects of child welfare most closely related to outdoor recreation. As a good citizen, she was also a strong supporter of civic improvement efforts of all kinds; though outdoor beautification projects were perhaps her specialty, she did not limit her efforts to these.

It began to be evident shortly before 1900 that the forest that residents of Michigan had though inexhaustible were nearly depleted.

> "...by 1870 the scene was set for the great logging and lumbering era of Michigan to get under way...billions of board feel of lumber were removed in the next thirty years...one measure suggests that it was enough to floor our entire state with one inch thick planks and have enough left over to floor Rhode Island as well. As the cutting continued through the 1870's and 1880's and 1890's, everyone still believed the forests were inexhaustible. They were not. By the end of the 19th century, the trees were gone..."[11]

Ella Sharp became a leader in the attempt to persuade the legislature to designate lands as forest preserves. Her efforts included writing an article on forestry in the 1905 Jackson Women's Magazine, a compilation of information about Jackson Women's Clubs and their interests. In this article, she described forestry as "the art of utilizing the forest and at the same time perpetuating it..."[12]

> Mrs. Sharp is recognized as the first woman in Michigan to take up the matter of forestry. This she did in her usual energetic, intelligent and practical way; brought it before the Women's Federation of the State; secured the first great petition to the governor; and thus, did more than anyone else to force this important subject to the

foreground with our administration of Michigan affairs.[13]

As a result of her effort, the legislature set aside new forest reserves, created a commission to study the situation, and established a definite fire patrol system in the state.

Ella Sharp did not stop with one victory. Over the next few years she carried on her work in this area, continuing her correspondence with Filibert Roth, State Forester and head of the Forestry Department at the University of Michigan, who wrote in a 1905 letter, "You will be needed there (Michigan Forestry Association Annual Meeting) to represent your very worthy self, the Federation and women of the state and to tell them of the good work done and going on."[14] At the Forestry Association's Fourth Annual Meeting held in Jackson in 1909, she spoke on "The Tree and Shrub in Civic Improvement Work."[15] Mrs. Sharp appears to be the only woman to address the Association during this period.

Her topic on that occasion neatly combined two of her chief interests. In the Michigan Federation of Women's Clubs, she had chaired the Civic and Town Improvement Committee as well as the Forestry Committee. She was a major force in forming the Jackson Town Improvement Society and served as its president from the time of its founding in 1902 until her death in 1912.

In 1869, Jackson had been described in one of its first city directories as a virtual paradise, "a magnificent city...possessing superior material advantages with exquisite homesteads and bustling businesses." While this flowery description may have satisfied the Jacksonians of the 1870's, Ella Sharp, "the doer," could not be satisfied if there were streets unswept, hospital rooms inadequately equipped, or children without books to read. The Town Improvement

Society undertook to make paradise comfortable, cultured and clean.

Sharp became very accustomed to speaking on the topic of civic improvement. "Mrs. Sharp is an entertaining speaker and has won not only a statewide but national reputation in her line of work", declared the Benton Harbor Civic League whom she was scheduled to address in 1911.[16] Not satisfied with what she already knew on this subject or any of her other interests, Mrs. Sharp picked up information leaflets and took numerous notes at the conference she attended. As chair of the Federation's Town and Civic Improvement Committee, she corresponded with clubs throughout the state about improvement projects. A young woman writing to her from the Bay City Young Women's Christian Association said, "Knowing you to be a general encyclopedia, I write you for information..."[17]

Sharp continued her pattern of traveling throughout her busy later years, not only attending conferences but taking numerous small trips and traveling to Europe in 1910. In June, 1911, she set out to tour the western states accompanied by two college girls. After a visit to Yellowstone National Park, the girls returned east, while the indefatigable Mrs. Sharp went on to Seattle and boarded a boat for Alaska. At stops along the way she admired the scenery, saw Indian villages, and purchased a large number of Indian baskets. She returned from her trip in August and added "An Alaskan Ramble" to the list of topics on which she was prepared to speak to various groups.

In the last years of her life, Ella Merriman Sharp was busy gathering more information on the causes and interests to which she was committed. She was appointed by Gov. Chase Osborn to represent Michigan at two national conferences. The first was the National Conservation Congress in Kansas City in the fall of 1911. the following spring she traveled to

St. Louis for the National Conference on Child Welfare. From both these conferences, she brought back piles of notes and printed material to enable her to share information with her fellow citizens. In 1912, only months before her death, she attended a conference on recreation in Cleveland at which one of the speakers declared,

> "The children of today give too much to passive amusements. They should be out in the air getting fresh air. This Association should combat every tendency on the part of youth to become high minded and passive."[18]

Ella Sharp's middle years had been marked by prolonged and bitter disputes over family wills. She sometimes found herself in the middle, as when her husband and her father disagreed over the disposition of her mother's and brother Howard's, estates. After the deaths of her father and her husband, Sharp had no very close relatives. Among her many cousins, friends and protegees, no one stood out as her logical heir. It is not surprising that she chose to leave the greatest part of her estate to the general public so that everyone could benefit and no one would be left out. Her will, written in 1908 following her husband's death, designated numerous small bequests and...

> "the remainder of my estate, both real and personal, I give and devise to the City of Jackson, in trust for the following purposes: To convert not less than 400 acres of my home farm...into a park to be know as the Ella W. Sharp Park and perpetually maintained for park purposes; The contents of my home...suitable for the nucleus of a museum which is my wish, shall be maintained in my farm home. To convert the balance of my estate into mon-

ey...perpetually invested and use the income thereof for beautifying and maintaining said property. It is my desire that all timber on the land be preserved as far as practical."[19]

Sharp died November 9, 1912 at the age of 55. Her legacy can be seen in the thriving forests of Michigan and in the beautiful public park and the private museum that bear her name in her city of Jackson. A monument dedicated to her memory stands near the park entrance. It was erected in 1928 by the Jackson Junior Chamber of Commerce. A bronze plaque on it reads: "This 630 acre tract and a generous endowment, the gift of Ella Wing Sharp to her native city of Jackson, 1912. Its beauty a fitting memorial to a useful life." Ella Wing Merriman Sharp, "the doer," would have liked that.

NOTES

[1] Moore's Rural New Yorker, 1865 clipping, Merriman Sharp Collection.

[2] Abraham Wing to Mary Merriman, October 16, 1859. Merriman-Sharp Collection, Ella Sharp Museum, Jackson, Michigan.

[3] Conway, Jill Ker, "Some Reflections on the History of Women's Organizations," Smith Alumnae Quarterly, p. 7-11, Winter, 1978.

[4] Michigan Female Seminary Sixth Annual Catalogue, 1872-73, p. 13.

[5] Catalogue, p. 13.

[6] Mary Merriman to Ella Sharp, April 21, 1886. Merriman-Sharp Collection.

[7] Mary Merriman to Ella Merriman, dated January 31, 1881. Merriman-Sharp Collection.

[8] Julia Parmalee to Ella Sharp, letter dated December 27, 1886. Merriman-Sharp Collection.

[9] Conway, p. 7-11.

[10] Carleton, Will, "That Swamp of Death, A City Ballad", Harper's Weekly, p. 1, September 17, 1881.

[11] Hosford, Karl, "Land Nobody Wants," Michigan Natural Resources Magazine, Vol. 52, No. 6, p. 54, Nov-Dec, 1983.

[12] Sharp, Mrs. John, "Michigan Forestry Problem," Jackson Woman's Magazine, p. 10, Spring, 1905. Merriman-Sharp Collection.

[13] "Mrs. J.C. Sharp in the Forestry Movement," The Patriot, November 24, 1907. Merriman-Sharp Collection.

[14] Filibert Roth to Ella Sharp, May 19, 1904. Merriman-Sharp Collection.

[15] Annual Meeting Program, Michigan Forestry Association, 1909. Merriman-Sharp Collection.

[16] Benton Harbor Civic League Announcement, April 18, 1911. Merriman-Sharp Collection.

[17] Mrs. A.W. Herrick to Ella Sharp, dated November 23, 1906. Merriman-Sharp Collection.

[18] "Say Rural Folk Need More Play," The Cleveland Plain Dealer, June 6, 1912. Merriman-Sharp Collection.

[19] Ella W. Sharp, "Last Will and Testament," August, 1908. Merriman-Sharp Collection.

CAROLINE BARTLETT CRANE (1858 – 1935)

CAROLINE BARTLETT CRANE:
MINISTER TO SICK CITIES

O'Ryan Rickard

Caroline Bartlett Crane's life was a quest for truth and purity in religious faith, a faith she applied in her church ministry and in civic service to her community, state, and nation. Remembered as both a minister of the social gospel and as an urban reformer, Crane was born in 1858 in Hudson, Wisconsin, into an environment of religious skepticism.[1] Her parents had resigned from a Methodist Church after its pastor had consoled them that it was "God's will" that two earlier children had died of scarlet fever. But Lorenzo and Julia Bartlett were not so sure of their lack of faith as to deprive their daughter of a religious education, and so they sent her to a Congregationalist Sunday School.

About 1865, Crane's father purchased a small river boat, The Viola, which carried passengers and freight on the Mississippi River. During summer vacation trips on the boat, Crane spent much of her time at the aft rail in solitary meditation about religious questions. Because of dwindling freight revenue, the boat was sold in 1874 and the family moved to Hamilton, Illinois. Soon after their arrival, Lorenzo arranged for a Unitarian minister to speak in town hall. The minister preached on "The Evolution of Religion," and Crane remembered that "in this sermon I found all my doubts and problems solved...it was like a message from heaven." Later that evening, she shocked her father with the news that she planned to become a Unitarian minister. Lorenzo Bartlett had invited the minister only to help his daughter resolve her doubts; it was unthinkable that she wanted to become a preacher herself.

But he was determined to provide her with a college education, and in 1876 she was admitted to Carthage College in Illinois. At that time, it was not uncommon for women's curricula at coeducational colleges to have less rigorous courses than the Calculus and Greek courses required for men to graduate. Crane refused to take the inferior women's course of study. She won her battle and completed the male curriculum, graduating as valedictorian in 1879.[2]

After graduation, she obtained a position as principal of the public school in Montrose, Iowa, but remained there only a year before returning to her parents' home to teach private elocution (a combination of public speaking, oral interpretation, and diction). In 1883, her mother died of gallstones, and in their mourning, father and daughter decided to move and file a homestead claim in Dakota.

During the winter of 1884, Crane left Dakota Territory and became a reporter for the Minneapolis Tribune.[3] A year later she accepted the position of city editor of the Oshkosh (Wisconsin) Morning Times but the ministry remained her goal.[4] So, in the spring of 1886 she returned to her father's home and finally obtained his permission. For the next six months, immersed in the treeless solitude of the Dakota prairie, Crane meditated and wrote out sermon-length answers to theological questions. Her early theology was flavored heavily with the transcendentalism of Ralph Waldo Emerson, who held that through mystical inner experiences men and women could come to know the universal God.[5] Although rejecting supernatural Christianity and Protestant orthodox doctrines of salvation, she believed in the existence of God in the Emersonian sense, the immortality of the soul, and the power of prayer.

Crane presented herself to the Iowa State Unitarian Conference meeting in Des Moines in the fall of 1886 and was accepted as a candidate for the ministry.[6] The Iowa Conference in the 1880s supplied the leadership in ordaining Unitarian women ministers, who were known as members of the "Iowa Sisterhood." Historians of religion point out that it was practical to ordain women in the West because they would serve small churches for smaller salaries than men, and it was difficult to attract male ministers to frontier situations.[7]

Crane became the pastor of the All Souls Unitarian Church in Sioux Falls, Dakota Territory, in January, 1887, and during her eighteen-month ministry there the congregation grew from about 70 members to 250 and a new church building was constructed.[8] In her first sermon in the new building, she expressed her belief in the Social Gospel, a Protestant theological response to the terrible social problems created by industrialism and the rapid growth of American cities. Along with many other Social Gospel preachers, she taught that humanity could create a better world or kingdom of heaven on earth, and that God lives through all the ranks of creation; therefore, He must dwell in the processes that give humanity moral ideals to improve society.[9] Like other Social Gospel advocates, she was influenced by Darwin's theory of evolution and used the theory to link moral and religious ideas to the contemporary optimistic belief in progress. Evolution's chief value, she believed, was not to explain the existence of life but to provide new understanding of the methods of life. In numerous sermons, she demonstrated the continuing evolution of humanity's moral understanding.[10]

In the fall of 1889, Crane assumed the pastorate of the First Unitarian Church in Kalamazoo, Michigan, a strife-ridden congregation which wanted a minister mainly to perform funerals.[11] The church membership grew and, with the help of a $20,000 gift, a new building was completed in December, 1894. This building gave life to a concept of the ministry Crane called the "seven day church," meaning that the church served the entire community every day, not just its own members on Sunday.[12] She convinced the congregation to change the name of the church to "People's Church," and to adopt her concept of a creedless "institutional" congregation devoted to social and educational programs for its members and for the community. By institutional, Crane meant that the church would inaugurate and demonstrate the value of innovative social programs to municipal governments and other civic institutions, which would then take on the projects. In 1899, Kalamazoo assumed control of a free public kindergarten previously operated by the church and church-operated schools of domestic science and manual training greatly influenced the city to initiate vocational skills education at the turn of the century.[13]

Similarly to settlement house programs, People's Church offered cultural opportunities such as lectures and studies in literature and the social sciences and a nature study group for children. Crane ardently believed that civic service was a moral and religious duty, especially imperative for church members because church properly was exempt from taxation. Under her leadership, the social science study group performed a sociological study of the city. During summer leave, Crane had taken two graduate courses in sociology at the University of Chicago, the site of the world's first department of sociology. She agreed with her instructors that society could be reformed through study.[14] She saw that small cities, such as Kalamazoo with its 20,000 population, had the same problems as larger metropolitan areas and felt they had the same social responsibility to their citizens.

Crane's ministry also extended to the poor, minorities, labor groups, and women. During the Panic of 1893, People's Church helped the city distribute food and clothing to the poor. One of her earliest successful crusades was the ousting of a callous county official who used abusive and racist language in his dealings with the poor and accepted kickbacks from local merchants.[15] Under her direction, a study club was organized for black women and she also helped to form a women's labor union in Kalamazoo.

Women labor organizers and suffragists spoke from the pulpit of People's Church, and in 1891, Crane spoke at the first of several conventions of the National American Woman Suffrage Association, which she served for several years as an executive board member.[16] In addition, she was a member of the board of directors of the Michigan Equal Suffrage Association and one of its most notable spokespersons in the fight for municipal suffrage.[17] One of the arguments she used was that women should be given the vote in local elections to fulfill their roles as municipal housekeepers.

Municipal housekeeping, the undertaking for which Crane is most remembered, originated in women's clubs in the East as early as the 1870s. Advocates of the concept maintained that women were naturally more suited than men for involvement in public health and other social issues which affected the family.[18] In 1893, Crane and suffragists Susan B. Anthony and Anna Howard Shaw addressed the Michigan legislature and a bill to give women the vote in local elections was enacted; however, the state supreme court ruled the law unconstitutional.[19] After that defeat, women in Michigan decided to forego the municipal suffrage strategy and seek full suffrage through public referenda and changes in the state constitution.[20]

In January, 1896, Caroline Bartlett Crane's ministry received national attention after it was erroneously reported that she had converted the "Great Heretic" Colonel Robert G. Ingersoll to Christianity.[21] During a lecture in Kalamazoo, Ingersoll had spoken highly of People's Church, saying that if he lived in the community, he would seek membership. The first press reports did not indicate that most of the orthodox Christians in the community thought the members of People's Church were themselves heretics. In his response to the press mistake, Ingersoll avoided affirming or denying reports on his comments, but briefly outlined the social work of the church and explained its creedlessness. He concluded his response by calling Crane "a remarkable person." Crane, too, took advantage of the mistake to publicize that the church was open to all people of good faith, and its current membership included liberal and orthodox Christians, Jews, Moslems, Christian Scientists, and Spiritualists. In her pulpit the following Sunday, Crane said that she preferred many of Ingersoll's beliefs to those of his critics and she argued that he should be extended membership to People's Church.[22]

Following the Ingersoll episode, Crane's ministry peaked. But in less than a year, her life style would change. Caroline Bartlett was thirty-eight-years-old when, to the surprise of most of her congregation, she married Dr. Augustus Warren Crane on New Year's Eve, 1896. Her husband, who was to become one of the nation's foremost pioneer radiologists, was ten years younger than she was. Crane's devotion to her many activities, a People's church, and to new home duties resulted in overwork and exhaustion. Citing poor health, she resigned her pastorate in June, 1898.[23] Although she had resigned her pastorate at People's Church, she did not resign from the ministry. She continued to preach frequently in other churches and became more devoted to civic service or what she called her "civic ministry." In her memoirs, Crane characterized her work in Dakota Territory and at People's

Church as her "church ministry" and her work as a social reformer as her "civic ministry."

In fact, the beginnings of Crane's civic ministry were evident in her work at People's Church, but it was 1901 before her reform work received attention beyond her home community. That year she led a group of prominent citizens on an inspection tour of the slaughterhouses in Kalamazoo and they found deplorable conditions.[24] Her local crusade led to the passage of a state law in 1903 that allowed cities and towns to enact ordinances controlling meat hygiene.[25] That same year she inspected the poorhouse conditions in Kalamazoo and embarked on another personal crusade to improve medical treatment for patients, most of whom were indigent elderly. She served as chairman of the 1906 convention of the Michigan State Conference of Charities and Corrections and County Agents and convinced that organization to endorse a plan to improve medical care in poorhouses. A survey of poorhouses by Crane's committee revealed no systematic health care. In most cases, only perfunctory annual examinations were performed. Under the plan approved by the convention, a joint committee of the Michigan State Federation of Women's Clubs and the Michigan State Nurses' Association sought cooperation with county officials in hiring nurses for the poorhouses.

Although she lobbied successfully on the state level, Crane's failure to get a meat inspection ordinance enacted in Kalamazoo and a nurse hired for the local poorhouse convinced her it was necessary to organize women in the community itself. In 1904, she persuaded thirteen women's organizations to establish the Women's Civic Improvement League of Kalamazoo.[26] Under Crane's leadership, the Kalamazoo League hired a nurse to visit the homes of the poor, advised women about such legal issues as divorce and widowhood, and held workshops on housekeeping and cooking skills.[27] The most important work of the League was performed by the Charity Organization Committee and the Public Health Committee. The Charity Organization Committee dispensed poor funds for the city, but only to those who could not work. Able-bodied unemployed men and women had to cut wood or sew to earn assistance. As chairman of the committee, Crane publicized how loan sharks preyed on the those with low incomes and convinced a bank to encourage small saving accounts for the poor.[28]

Crane also served as chairwoman of the Public Health Committee and led the Civic Improvement League in an experimental project to improve the cleanliness of downtown streets. This project gained national attention in the press.[29] Adopting a system created by a New York sanitation engineer, sanitation workers wearing white uniforms patrolled the downtown area with pushbrooms, and at night firemen washed down the streets. Crane herself frequently rose at 3:00 a.m. to direct the firemen on the proper technique.

In 1906, Upton Sinclair's The Jungle created an uproar over poor sanitary conditions in the Chicago stockyards, and Crane was asked by the special investigator for President Theodore Roosevelt to critique revised federal meat inspection regulations. She found that the revised rules did little to improve the quality of meat served on the American dinner table, and she objected to the new regulations on the grounds they would continue to allow federal approval of meat infected with such diseases as the very common bovine tuberculosis. In addition, the rules covered only meats shipped between states.

Crane secretly was given United States Department of Agriculture (USDA) internal documents called "Service Announcements" that she claimed revealed a conspiracy between the meatpackers and the federal inspectors to weaken enforcement of meat inspection regulations. She disclosed the existence of the documents at the American Public Health Association convention in 1909, and asked that group to investigate her allegations. It refused, according to Crane, because of pressure from the United States Department of Agriculture (USDA).[30] During the next three years, she continued her research and in 1912, her allegations were again aired before the House Committee on Expenditures in the Department of Agriculture.[31] Meatpackers hurried to Washington to apply pressure on committee members, and the USDA initiated a smear campaign against Crane, distributing documents that claimed she had been paid by special interests to investigate meatpacking conditions.[32] USDA officials claimed Crane knew little about meat inspection methods, but Dr. Harvey W. Wiley, former chief chemist of the Department of Agriculture and the leader of the pure food movement, said that Crane was one of the "highest authorities" on meat inspection in America.[33] Although Crane's testimony besmirched the reputation of the USDA's meat inspection enforcement force, the hearings did not lead to major reforms during her lifetime. It was 1967 before all meat was covered by federal inspection and 1972 before the USDA banned the sale of all meat infected with tuberculosis.[34]

Meanwhile, Crane earned the titles "minister to cities," and "America's public housekeeper" by making investigations of social and sanitary conditions in sixty-two American cities between 1907 and 1916.[35] Her investigative technique was based on the model of the sociological survey, stressing critical examination of municipal services and hygiene. Crane called herself a "municipal sanitarian," and her investigations were known as "Sociological and Sanitary Surveys." Her method of investigation was a systematic but personal observation of the elements that make up city life--the water supplies, sewers, street sanitation, garbage collection and disposal, milk and meat supplies, bakeries, food factories, schoolhouses, poorhouses, hospitals, prisons, and institutions of detention for the poor, elderly, orphans, and the mentally ill. She demanded community-wide support for her work prior to her arrival for a "sanitary survey," but she frequently met opposition after revealing the results of her investigation. Most commonly her sponsors were local or state boards of health, city officials, women's clubs, chambers of commerce, associations of physicians, and civic-minded community organizations. In Saginaw, Michigan, for example, Crane was invited to make a survey by twenty-two cooperating organizations.[36] She was usually paid $300 to $400 for a single-city survey and as much as $1,500 for a multi-city statewide investigation.

Using her experience as a journalist and her talent as a public speaker, Crane had press releases ready for journalists when she arrived in a city and made a public speech describing her findings, both favorable and unfavorable, at the conclusion of her survey. On several occasions, her disclosures were published as a guideline for reform in a community.[37]

Crane also tackled civic improvement on a statewide level. In 1909, she conducted an investigation in Kentucky, examining conditions in twelve cities where she was hailed as an "apostle of civic righteousness."[38] Her greatest challenge, however, was a seventeen-city survey of Minnesota in 1910. Although her work stressed sanitation and urban reform, she also spoke out against injustice and inhumane social conditions. Among her many accomplishments as America's public housekeeper, Crane listed the construction of new poorhouses and hospitals, improved sanitation conditions, new laws, and the creation of twenty civic improvement leagues.[39]

At the age of 55, Crane and her husband adopted two infants, and during the next two years, she reduced her public commitments to take care of the children. But after the

United State entered World War I in the spring of 1917, Crane was appointed President of the Michigan Women's Committee of National Defense and the time devoted to her public life increased. The Federal Administration created the National Woman's Committee to organize the women for defense work. Anna Howard Shaw, who had stepped down as NAWSA president in 1915, was named national chairperson, and she appointed Crane to the Michigan leadership post.[40] During the brief existence of the Michigan Women's Committee, 900,000 women were registered for volunteer wartime service and campaigns were organized to conserve food and improve infant mortality. Patriotic work by Shaw, Crane, and other suffragists was instrumental in gaining public sentiment for the passage of the federal suffrage amendment. For the first time, Crane, at the age of sixty-two, was able to vote in a national election.[41]

During the 1920s, Crane became known as a housing reformer and was an associate editor of the Woman's Journal, a prestigious magazine for civic-minded women.[42] With a great deal of foresight, she wrote and lectured on the dangers of future sprawling urban developments, stressing the need for housing laws to cover small cities and yet-to-be developed suburban areas.[43] One high point for Crane in the 1920s was her winning entry in the national "Better Homes in America Contest," a movement to encourage the development of new family housing. She called her design "Everyman's House" because working class persons could afford it, but it was really a "woman's house" with several features to help young housewives take care of their children.[44]

Although the period after 1925 was one of decreasing activism for Caroline Bartlett Crane, she never lost her faith in humanity's ability to improve society. She campaigned for the creation of local and state prison farms, served on the national boards of the National Municipal League and the

American Civic Association, and in 1933, was named the chairman of the Michigan Association for Old Age Security.

Crane died of a heart attack at her home in Kalamazoo in 1935 and was eulogized for her selfless service to her community, state and nation.[45] In 1985, her importance to women's history was recognized by her induction into the Michigan Women's Hall of Fame. Her individual accomplishments as a social gospel preacher; suffragist; and urban, social, housing and meat hygiene reformer were substantial. In the diversity of her activism, Caroline Bartlett Crane provides a panorama of women's contributions from the 1880s to the 1930s.

NOTES

[1] Caroline Bartlett Crane, unpublished autobiographical sketches, ca. 1934, Crane Papers, Western Michigan University Archives and Regional History Collections, Kalamazoo, Michigan. Unless otherwise specified, the autobiographical material in this essay is taken from these recollections.

[2] Carthage College 1879 Graduation Program, Crane Papers.

[3] "The Pastor and the People's Church: Recollections of Her as a Newspaper Worker in Minneapolis by her City Editor," Cincinnati Commercial-Gazette, 2 February 1896, Nell Hudson Scrapbooks, Crane Papers.

[4] Oshkosh Morning Times, Wisconsin State Historical Society, Madison, Wisconsin.

[5] Caroline J. Bartlett, "Natural or Revealed Religion," a sermon delivered 21 October 1888, Sioux Falls, Dakota Territory (Yankton, Dakota Territory: Press and Dakotian Print, 1888), p. 6.

[6] Program of the Iowa Unitarian Association Conference, 1886, Crane Papers.

[7] Catherine Hitchings, Universalist and Unitarian Women Ministers (Boston: Universalist Historical Society, 1975) pp. 4-5.

[8] "Once a Reporter," Minneapolis Tribune, 25 May 1889, clipping in Crane Papers.

[9] Charles Howard Hopkins, The Rise of the Social Gospel in American Protestantism 1865-1915 (New Haven, Conn.: Yale University Press, 1940), p. 318.

[10] Bartlett, "Natural or Revealed Religion," p. 5.

[11] Crane, "The Story of an Institutional Church in a Small City," Charities and the Commons 14 (May 6, 1905): 723-731.

[12] Church Minutes, Board of Trustees, 23 April 1984, People's Church Library Archives.

[13] Minutes of the Kalamazoo Board of Education from 1882-1901, p. 641, Kalamazoo Board of Education Administration Building, Kalamazoo, Michigan.

[14] University of Chicago class notebooks, Crane Papers.

[15] "The Supervisors Committee Report Against Superintendent Bush," Kalamazoo Gazette, 17 January 1896.

[16] Susan B. Anthony and Ida Husted Harper, eds., The History of Woman Suffrage, Vol. 4 (Rochester, N.Y.: Source Book Press, Susan B. Anthony, 1902) p. 184.

[17] Virginia Ann Paganelli Caruso, A History of Woman Suffrage in Michigan, doctoral dissertation, Michigan State University, 1986, p. 104.

[18] Karen J. Blair, The Clubwoman as Feminist: True Womanhood Redefined, 1868-1914 (New York, London: Holmes and Meier Publishers, Inc. 1980) pp. 73-74.

[19] Anthony and Harper, The History of Woman Suffrage, Vol. 4, p. 764.

[20] Caruso, A History of Woman Suffrage in Michigan, p. 118-119.

[21] "Have the Prayers Been Answered?" New York Journal,

13 January 1896; "Its Deeds Suit Ingersoll," Chicago Chronicle, 17 January 1896.

[22]"Ingersoll's Church," New York Journal, 16 January 1896.

[23]Church Minutes, Board of Trustees, 27 May 1898, People's Church.

[24]"Foul Places," Kalamazoo Evening Telegraph, 25 March 1902.

[25]Michigan Legislature, "An Act to Provide for the Inspection of Animals Intended for Meat Supplies," Public Acts, 1903, Act 120, pp. 140-143.

[26]Mabel Potter Daggett, "One Woman's Civic Service," Delineator 73 (June 1909) p. 819.

[27]Suellen M. Hoy, "Municipal Housekeeping: The Role of Women in Improving Urban Sanitation Practices, 1880-1917," in Pollution and Reform in American Cities 1870-1930, ed., Martin V. Melosi (Austin, Tex.: University of Texas Press, 1980) pp. 174-178.

[28]"Strong Organizations Aim Death-Blow at Loan Sharks," undated Kalamazoo newspaper clipping, Crane Papers.

[29]"Michigan Women are Making a Spotless Town," New York Herald, 8 May 1904, Crane Papers.

[30]"Documentary Evidence Produced by Mrs. Crane," The News Leader (Richmond and Manchester, VA) 21 October 1909; and U.S. Department of Agriculture, Bureau of Animal Industry, several Service Announcements, photographic copies, Crane Papers.

[31]U.S. House of Representatives, Proceedings of Hearings before the Committee on Expenditures in the Department of Agriculture on Nelson Resolution 51, 1912, p. 8, microfilm reproduction in Detroit, Michigan, City Library.

[32]"Oppose Meat Inquiry," New York Times, 2 May 1912 and Harvey W. Wiley, "The Attack on Caroline Bartlett Crane," Good Housekeeping 55 (July 1912) pp. 107-108.

[33]"Wiley Upholds Woman in Beef Test Charges," New York Sun, 10 May 1912, Crane Papers.

[34]Interview with Clarence Pals, 7 September 1985. Pals was head of the federal meat inspection service from 1960 to 1965 and is considered by the USDA as the best historical source on meat inspection.

[35]Notable American Women: A Biographical Dictionary, s.v. Caroline Bartlett Crane," by Charles Starring, Cambridge, Mass: Harvard University Press, 1971, pp. 401-402.

[36]Caroline Bartlett Crane, Sanitary Survey of Saginaw, Michigan, n. p., 1911, Crane Papers.

[37]Reports of Crane's surveys were published in Erie, Pennsylvania; Saginaw, Michigan; Nashville, Tennessee; Rochester, New York; Uniontown, Pennsylvania, and her survey of Minnesota resulted in a 224-page examination of her statewide investigation.

[38]"Mrs. Crane's Work in Kentucky," Kentucky Medical Journal 7 (1 August 1909), p. 601.

[39]Helen Christine Bennett, "Caroline Bartlett Crane" in American Women in Civic Work, (New York: Dodd, Mead and Company, 1915), pp. 41-42.

[40]Crane, History of the Work of the Women's Committee (Michigan Division) Council of National Defense During the World War (Lansing, Michigan: State Administrative Office, 1922) p. 6.

[41]J. Stanley Lemons, The Woman Citizen: Social Feminism in the 1920s, (Urbana, Ill, University of Illinois Press, 1973), p. 4,10.

[42]"Dr. C.B. Crane Is Named On Staff Of N.Y. Magazine," Kalamazoo Gazette, 12 April 1925, Crane Papers.

[43]Caroline Bartlett Crane, "Small Town Tenements," Woman Citizen n.s. 10 August 1925) p. 11; Crane, "Suburbs Beyond the Law," Woman Citizen n.s. 10 (September 1925) p. 12.

[44] Blanche Brace, "A Home Built Around a Mother," *Delineator* (February 1912), p. 2.; and Caroline Bartlett Crane, *Everyman's House* (Garden City, N.Y.: Doubleday, Page & Company, 1925).

[45] "Caroline Bartlett Crane," *New York Times*, 25 March 1935.

BERTHA VAN HOOSEN (1863 – 1952)

BERTHA VAN HOOSEN
SURGEON

Clara Raven, M.D.

Editor's Note: Instead of a reseach essay, Dr. Raven has written a personal remembrance of her friend and colleague. A different version of this essay appeared in the Journal of the American Medical Women's Association, *Volume 18, Number 7, July, 1963.*

It seems as though I have always known Dr. Bertha Van Hoosen. Actually, I first met her at a student tea given by the Chicago branch of the Women's Medical Association in 1933. I was then a sophomore at Northwestern University Medical School. Dr. Van Hoosen was professor and chairman of the Department of Obstetrics and Gynecology at Loyola University Medical School.

There was something magnetic about her personality. I never learned why she became interested in me. Perhaps it was because I, too, was an alumnus of the University of Michigan; perhaps it was because she recognized my dogged determination to study medicine regardless of the depression-geared poverty of the 1930's; perhaps it was because of her interest in my background in bacteriology and contagious diseases. She was quick to recognize that I was serious and dedicated and those qualitites interested her, I believe. I saw her occasionally as a student and more frequently later when I was an intern and she on the attending staff at the Women and Children's Hospital in Chicago. I gradually came to look upon her as a loyal friend and counselor. Conversation with her was a revelation. Her experiences fascinated me and were a constant source of inspiration.

She loved to talk about her family, her beloved sister Alice and her niece, Sarah Van Hoosen Jones, who lived on the old Van Hoosen homestead, in Rochester, Michigan. Her vivid descriptions of the large farm were so real that years later, when I finally visited it, I could recognize some of the landmarks. I also felt that I knew Sarah Jones as an old friend. How "Dr. Van" must have hoped that her niece would study medicine; however, she was not one to impose her will on anyone. Although a dreamer, she was a realist par excellence. When her niece decided to study agriculture, Dr. Van was there rooting for her, confident that she would be a top-notch farmer. She lived to glory in the many honors bestowed upon her niece in her chosen field. With the aid of Dr. Van Hoosen, Sarah Jones carried on many experiments on the Van Hoosen farms; she became known as a Master Farmer and served often as a national consultant. She was one of the first to produce Vitamin D enriched milk and won many trophies for prize cattle and poultry.

Many of Dr. Van's inspirations and ideas in her medical career came from her experiences on the farm. It was there she was first exposed to life and death, to birth, biology, and zoology. I remember how she once explained to her class her first experience with the stages of labor and birth in animals. Down-to-earth examples such as these made her an effective and beloved teacher. Physicians who had been her students never forgot her teachings, especially those which were not available in textbooks.

Dr. Van Hoosen was far ahead of her time in many things. It was her belief, for instance, that since the animals devoured their afterbirths, there must be some beneficial substance in the placental tissue. She, therefore, had prepared for her an extract to be administered to nursing mothers in some instance of inadequate lactation. She also insisted that all the babies she delivered be breast-fed. So convinced was she of the importance of breast feeding that she started a human breast-milk bank in the City of Chicago. This was particularly valuable for premature infants and others with natal deficiencies. She was also convinced as to the importance of good maternal nutrition during pregnancy. She was particularly adamant on not drinking, smoking, or taking unnecessary medicines during pregnancy. The importance of this precaution has only recently been recognized by the entire profession.

She was constantly on the alert for new ideas, regardless of where they came from. A traumatic experience which had an indelible influence on her career came to her within her own family. She attended her sister Alice during a very prolonged and difficult labor for the birth of her niece Sarah, born lifeless and saved by her miraculous resuscitation. It was perhaps this episode which influenced her in her research into ways to alleviate painful labor. In 1909 she published a treatise on "Twilight Sleep" and championed scopolamine morphine as a salvation for difficult labor. She presented her researches to an international congress in Europe. This treatment was later modified, but the concept persists to this day.

Bertha Van Hoosen had a great concern for cancer patients. She became firmly convinced that breast cancer was due to an infectious agent, perhaps similar to a protozoan infection, so she decided to try emetine hydrochloride. Of course, large doses were prohibitive because of the toxicity. So she traveled to England and made special arrangements with Burroughs-Welcome to produce a less toxic agent. I personally saw some of her experimental animal material and witnessed the treatment of several patients. Although there were no cures, there was evidence of local destruction of the tumors.

She was also constantly looking for improvements in her surgical technique. Frequent trips to surgical centers in Europe were often rewarded with new procedures such as the buttonhole incision for appendectomy.

My own premedical and medical environment had been dominated by men. It was not until I reached my internship at the Women and Children's Hospital in Chicago that I was exposed to a predominance of women in medicine. It was an exhilarating and stimulating experience. Dr. Van Hoosen had been gradually building up for me the concept of the importance of women in medicine. It was during my internship that I was able to see the work of women at close range. It was my privilege to work in close contact with Pearl Mae Stetler, Marie Ortmayer, Eloise Parsons, and many others.

Also during my internship, I learned Dr. Van's concept of patient care. With her it was a holy trust, and she constantly impressed me with the great responsibility the physician should have for her patient. In her autobiography, Petticoat Surgeon, published in 1947, she says, "Perhaps, after all, in my choice of a medical career, unconsciously I was responding to a call of the woman in me--woman, preserver of the race--to mitigate suffering and save life."[1]

In a forward to Petticoat Surgeon, Dr. A.E. Hertzler said that she had proved to the world that a woman can achieve first rank in surgery. Sometimes her concern for patients caused administrative difficulties. For instance, her regimen for her patients had to be strictly adhered to and was under her rigid control. She liked to begin her surgery at 7:30 a.m. sharp and we had to be scrubbed and ready around the operating table at 7:00 a.m. As an intern, it was my responsibility to check the patient and the preoperative medications at 5:00 a.m. and subsequently at half-hour intervals, charting blood pressure, pulse, and respirations, and reporting to her any abnormalities. On her obstetrical patients, scopolamine sedation was most carefully controlled and individualized. The patient was under continual surveillance from the time the first dose was given.

In her hospital management, Dr. Van reminded me of Dr. George Crile, the famous thyroid surgeon in Cleveland. During a visit when I made ward rounds with him, he told us his teamwork and regimentation was patterned after his World War I experiences in surgery. Like him, Dr. Bertha Van Hoosen was a true soldier and believer in regimentation.

Not only did Dr. Van Hoosen stimulate my interest in the American Medical Women's Association (AMWA), which she had founded, but she also made me aware of the power of women in the social and technical sciences related to medicine. She introduced me to Hull House, the center of social reform in Chicago; to the Chicago Mental Hygiene Clinic and its head Dr. Rachel Yarros, an exponent of birth control and planned parenthood; and to the Chicago Cradle, which arranged for scientific adoptions of foundlings. She also made me aware of other national and international women who were leaders in the medical profession, and later I became acquainted with many of them.

After my return from a year of postgraduate research and study in England and while teaching at the Woman's Medical College of Pennsylvania, I felt it my duty to volunteer for service in the U.S. Army at the beginning of World War II. It was Dr. Van Hoosen who advised me as to the course to take. Actually, her war experience occurred during World War I, when, as the first president of the American Women's Medical Association, she organized a war service committee. When I was finally commissioned, she followed my movements overseas in Europe and later in Japan during the Korean War.

My premedical background and research training logically legislated my career in pathology; however, I have often wished that I could have been one of Bertha Van Hoosen's surgical daughters. I felt that something precious had left this world when I learned of her death in 1952.

NOTES

[1] Bertha Van Hoosen, Petticoat Surgeon, (Chicago: People's Book Club, 1947), p. 55.

VOLTAIRINE DE CLEYRE (1866 - 1912)

VOLTAIRINE DE CLEYRE
SOCIAL VISIONARY

Blaine McKinley

Voltairine de Cleyre was an American-born anarchist and feminist who grew up in St. Johns, Michigan. Although she is seldom remembered today, 2000 people attended the ceremony at her burial when she died in Chicago at the premature age of 45. As an anarchist, de Cleyre believed that all authority external to the individual was oppressive, that all forms of political and economic organization should be strictly voluntary in nature, and that cooperative institutions and individual self-control would produce harmony in a society founded on personal freedom.[1]

De Cleyre contradicted the popular stereotype of the anarchist as a bloodthirsty, foreign-born bomb thrower. Her vision of a decentralized society based on individual liberty and voluntary cooperation owed more to her small-town upbringing and the American traditions of suspicion of government and reliance on individual initiative than it did to European radical theories. Nor did she throw bombs. De Cleyre did sympathize with anarchists, such as Alexander Berkman or the Italian Michele Angiolillo, who carried out acts of political violence, because she regarded them as sensitive men driven to their desperate acts by injustice. She took no part in such violent activities, however; instead, she relied upon the peaceful methods of education and persuasion to bring about a change in American values. Her single arrest, on a charge of inciting a riot in Philadelphia, resulted in an acquittal when no prosecution witness appeared to testify against her.

De Cleyre was born in Leslie, Michigan, in 1866 and was named for Voltaire, whom her father admired. The next year the family moved to St. Johns, residing at 204 South Lansing Street. The house, which still stands, remained in the family until 1945 when de Cleyre's sister, Adelaide D. Thayer, a former school teacher in St. Johns, died.

Young Voltairine's parents (who spelled the family name De Claire) were unhappily married, a situation worsened by the family's extreme poverty. Her parents separated when de Cleyre was small; her father, a tailor, moved to Port Huron, while her mother and the two daughters remained in St. Johns. As a child, de Cleyre became an avid reader and delighted in her pet animals and birds. She attended the St. Johns public schools until she was 12. When she was 13, her father sent her to a convent school in Sarnia, Ontario, which he had selected for his precocious but headstrong daughter, both because he thought she needed discipline and because of the excellent education it would provide.

De Cleyre endured a difficult time at the convent school. She went through a period of religious questioning and felt both attracted to and repelled by the Catholic religious imagery and the regularity and order of convent life. She chafed under the rules of the school, and in later life she interpreted her anarchism as a personal rebellion against the lingering impact of the convent's rigid discipline. Nonetheless, she did well in her studies, and at graduation in 1883 she won a gold medal, which she frequently wore even after becoming an anarchist. Following graduation, she returned to St. Johns for two years, giving private lessons in music and French.

De Cleyre's life turned toward radicalism when she left her mother's home in 1885 and moved first to Greenville, Michigan, and then to Grand Rapids. She became involved in the free thought movement and began to lecture throughout southern Michigan on the evils of dogmatism and rigid authority in religious matters. As the attractive young lecturer became more experienced, she traveled as far as Boston and Kansas to speak for free thought groups. Her rejection of religious control led de Cleyre to a more sweeping attack on all forms of authority and all restrictions on individual liberty. By 1888 she had adopted the cause of anarchism. This lifelong commitment was reinforced by her identification with the Haymarket martyrs, executed in 1887 for their alleged involvement in Chicago's Haymarket Square bombing the preceding year.

In 1889 Voltairine de Cleyre moved to Philadelphia, where she lived until 1910. In Philadelphia she made a modest living as a private teacher giving English lessons to immigrant Jewish laborers. Although her income was small, she saved enough, through frugality and self-denial, to put a lover through medical school and to send small but regular amounts to her mother in St. Johns. De Cleyre moved to Chicago in 1910; there she continued her work as a tutor of Jewish immigrants until her death.

De Cleyre spoke often in the Philadelphia area and was a well-known figure at labor, radical, and free thought meetings. She also spoke in other cities, especially Chicago, which she visited almost yearly, and she made two lecture tours of Great Britain, where she fell in love with the beauties of Scotland. As a writer, de Cleyre contributed poems, essays, and short stories to a variety of radical publications. One of her abiding interests was history, particularly American history, and historical references pepper her essays. Her best-known essay, "Anarchism and American Traditions," tries to demonstrate that anarchism had deep roots in the American experience and was not an exotic foreign importation. The article traces similarities between the ideals of the anarchists and those of the Revolutionary fathers of 1776, especially Thomas Jefferson. According to de Cleyre, both groups sought to decentralize power and minimize the authority of government, and both based their beliefs on the fundamental principle that "equal liberty is the political ideal."[2]

Another of her interests was language. De Cleyre knew German and was fluent in French, even translating a French anarchist book into English. She also laboriously taught herself to read and write Yiddish, the language of her immigrant pupils. Her love of language and its effects shows itself in her poetry, which she began to write as a child. A book of her poems appeared in 1900, but her poetic style is too florid and didactic for modern tastes. Her best poems are tributes to anarchist heroes such as the Haymarket martyrs.[3]

Friends used terms such as generous, stubborn, self-denying, and pessimistic to describe her complex personality. One of her dominant characteristics was fierce independence and hatred of feeling obligated to others. She described herself in a letter to her mother as "a rather cold, self-reliant sort of an individual, looking for help from nobody and given to biting my lips a good deal."[4] A reserved, introverted woman, de Cleyre always cherished her privacy and treasured secluded times alone without disturbing intrusions.

She was also defiant, but could include a touch of humor in her challenges to authority. When a United States senator offered $1000 for a chance to shoot an anarchist in 1902, de Cleyre called his bluff by offering herself as a target. She sent her response, including her address and a promise to stand still and not resist, to an anarchist paper. Moreover, she chided the senator that she was willing to serve as a target free of charge, "a bargain" she was certain a good capitalist would not want to miss.[5]

Later that same year, a real assassin challenged her anarchist convictions. A deluded former pupil named Herman Helcher, who suffered paranoid fantasies that de Cleyre was rejecting his unspoken love and persecuting him, shot her three times at point-blank range. Helcher wounded her severely, one bullet lodging near de Cleyre's heart. Consistent with her beliefs that crime was caused by mental illness and social oppression, and that, therefore, traditional punishment was inappropriate for criminals, de Cleyre refused to press charges against Helcher and even helped to raise money for her assailant's defense. True to her principles, she argued that he should be hospitalized as insane rather than imprisoned as a criminal.

De Cleyre endured other physical pain as well. She was plagued by chronic sinus inflammations and suffered daily, agonizing pain for much of her life. The pain in her throat often prevented her from speaking above a whisper, and "a continual pounding noise in her head" sometimes made concentration impossible for weeks at a time.[6] Her death in 1912 resulted from a severe sinus infection which caused an inflammation of the middle ear. The disease entered her brain, and she died after two operations and nine weeks of terrible pain.

Partly because of her chronic illness, de Cleyre was subject to prolonged periods of despair and severe depression. During these times, moods of what she called "terrible apathy" and "mental stupor" came over her and she experienced grave doubts about her beliefs, but her strength of character and will ultimately always enabled her to persevere in spite of physical and mental anguish.[7] As a coworker for the anarchist cause noted in a memorial tribute, "Her character became great through suffering and in spite of suffering."[8]

De Cleyre's significance lies in courageously living her life as she chose and in boldly questioning Victorian convention and the age's uncritical optimism about the course of American development. One need not share her anarchist convictions to respect her courage in asking significant questions which many people chose to ignore. At the very center of her thinking was the core belief that "the object of life should be the development of individuality."[9] All her other principles flowed from her conviction that every man and woman should pursue personal growth rather than blindly follow social convention. She taught, and lived by, the premise that each individual should strive for independence and self-reliance.

Her emphasis on individual growth made de Cleyre an ardent feminist. Male domination became yet another form of authority restraining human liberty. She felt "a bitter, passionate sense of personal injustice" at women's subordinate status, and she concluded "that the assumptions as to woman's inferiority were all humbug; that given freedom of opportunity, women were just as responsive as men, just as capable of making their own way, producing as much for the social good as men."[10] Her feminism often seems very modern, as when she called upon parents to overcome the gender stereotypes preventing young girls from playing sports and young boys from playing with dolls.[11]

Her harshest feminist criticism fell on the traditional nuclear family, which allegedly made men and women dependent rather than independent. Conventional family life, de Cleyre argued, stifled the development of "the free individual" and thus limited "the growth of both parties," particularly the woman, who became an economically dependent servant. Furthermore, she found marriage to be an unsatisfactory choice for infatuated young adults. Because people continued to change throughout their lives, she suggested, two partners could not remain equally compatible over an entire lifetime together. Marriage thus guaranteed most people only dependence, frustration, and unhappiness.[12]

In place of pinning their hopes on the elusive dream of an ideal marriage, de Cleyre called upon women to assert themselves and to strive toward emotional and economic independence. Women should claim their own identities and overcome the socialization and passivity which had made them emotionally dependent. Equally important was the right to economic "self-maintenance" because "the basis of independence and of individuality is bread."[13]

In her personal life as well, de Cleyre was, as one historian states, "a thoughtful and unconventional woman attempting to transcend the limitations of traditional femininity."[14] Because of her fiercely independent nature, she refused to marry or even to share a home with any man; this rejection of a conventional home life made her love relationships stormy and unhappy. As de Cleyre wrote to one lover from England, she was determined to retain "individual ownership" of herself and remain "a free woman" at all costs rather than live with him and thereby "suffer the tortures of owning and being owned."[15] De Cleyre's biographer, Paul Avrich, states her position clearly: "Asserting her independence as a person, as the possessor of her own body and mind, she rejected the traditional role of mother and household drudge, subject to the dictates of a husband."[16] De Cleyre, whose only child was born out of wedlock, understood the great personal costs of her unconventional decisions, but she never regretted refusing to compromise her individuality.

Not only women were denied individual development, according to de Cleyre. She contended that an unjust economic system based on monopoly capitalism and entrenched wealth restricted economic opportunity and impoverished and brutalized the laboring classes. Workers should, therefore, strive to win free access to productive resources and to erase the "great disparity in possessions between class and class." In this way, the laborer could throw off the chains forged by exploitation and reclaim his "individual dignity." As an anarchist, de Cleyre argued that political action was unable to achieve justice for workers because it "destroys initiative" and makes them dependent on politicians and government. Instead, workers should utilize the strike to win their right to "independent manhood" because "their power lies in their ability to stop production." In the economic area, as in others, de Cleyre's goal was "to allow every one to be able to stand upon his [or her] own feet."[17]

To de Cleyre, individualism was further endangered by the growing bureaucracy and centralization of American life. Although she lived in Philadelphia and Chicago, de Cleyre's vision remained a product of her childhood in St. Johns. She retained such small-town values as local autonomy and individual responsibility. De Cleyre frequently visited her mother in St. Johns when going to or returning from speaking engagements, but her feelings about the town she had grown up in were ambivalent. Writing to her mother in 1907, she compared St. Johns to Oliver Goldsmith's lamented "Deserted Village"--"so very pretty, but dead."[18] If her reaction to her home town was divided, she consistently despised large cities, regarding them as places of dirt, poverty, crime, and suffering. In one essay, she referred to cities as "rot-heaps of humanity. . ., where every filthy thing is done, and filthy labor breeds filthy bodies and filthy souls."[19] More directly, and more colloquially, when her mother wrote de Cleyre that she thought Buffalo, New York, "a beautiful city," de Cleyre retorted "all cities are vile; them's my sentiments."[20]

Like Thomas Jefferson, whom she often quoted, de Cleyre hoped for a return to local autonomy and local self-sufficiency. She worried, as did other anarchists, that the

Voltairine de Cleyre 151

consolidation of industrial capitalism and growth of powerful national institutions would erode the liberty and self-reliance prevalent in an earlier America. Men and women of vision and resolve, she thought, must resist the intrusions of paternalistic, centralized bureaucracies—whether religious, political, or economic—which claimed the right to control Americans. To de Cleyre, the good society was decentralized, a society where political and economic control rested in local communities. She desired the breakup of huge cities and huge factories and envisioned in their places "thousands of small communities stretching along the lines of transportation, each producing very largely for its own needs, able to rely upon itself, and therefore able to be independent."[21] For de Cleyre, only a self-sufficient community could be truly free.

Modern industrialism had brought not only the evils of urbanization and centralization but also the disease of "Thing-Worship." De Cleyre castigated modern Americans for having no higher aim than producing and possessing things—"things ugly, things harmful, things useless, and at the best largely unnecessary." She followed Henry David Thoreau in pleading with people "to renounce the worthless luxuries which enslave them" and to adopt a life of simplicity in place of crass materialism. Both de Cleyre and Thoreau defined the good life, the free life, as one founded on frugality and self-reliance. Both called upon Americans to pursue the ideals of the mind and spirit and reject what de Cleyre called the modern "rush and jangle of the chase for wealth."[22]

Although in many ways de Cleyre succeeded in rebelling against her convent education, she remained basically a moralist calling for a change of heart and values. If her behavior and life choices sometimes strike us as odd, it is because she courageously attempted to live by her personal values of liberty rather than by the conventions of her day or ours. Challenging people to question not only their society but also themselves, de Cleyre asks them to become active, to develop their individuality, to take control of their own lives, and to assume personal responsibility for their decisions. Her message to her generation, and to ours, is well stated in the following advice: "Be yourself; and by self-expression learn self-restraint."[23]

NOTES

[1] Any consideration of Voltairine de Cleyre's life and work must begin with Paul Avrich's fine biography, An American Anarchist: The Life of Voltairine de Cleyre (Princeton, N.J.: Princeton University Press, 1978).

[2] Voltairine de Cleyre, Selected Worked of Voltairine de Cleyre, ed. Alexander Berkman (New York: Mother Earth Publishing Association, 1914), pp. 118-135. "Anarchism and American Traditions" has been reprinted in Henry J. Silverman, ed., American Radical Thought: The Libertarian Tradition (Lexington, Mass.: D.C. Heath, 1970); Laurence Veysey, ed., Law and Resistance: American Attitudes Toward Authority (New York: Harper and Row, 1970); and Wendy McElroy, ed., Freedom, Feminism, and the State: An Overview of Individualist Feminism (Washington, D.C.: Cato Institute, 1982).

[3] Many of her poems appear in Selected Works, pp. 17-75.

[4] De Cleyre to Harriet De Claire, June 26, 1897, Labadie Collection, Department of Rare Books and Special Collections, University of Michigan Library.

[5] Avrich, American Anarchist, p. 136.

[6] Nathan Navro, Manuscript on Voltairine de Cleyre, Joseph Ishill Papers, by permission of the Houghton Library, Harvard University, p. 21.

[7] De Cleyre to Saul Yanovsky, March 29, 1911, Ishill Papers. Also quoted in Avrich, p. 224.

[8] Leonard D. Abbott, "Voltairine de Cleyre's Posthumous Book," Mother Earth, Vol. 9 (October 1914), p. 269.

[9] De Cleyre, "They Who Marry Do Ill," Mother Earth, Vol. 2 (January 1908), p. 505.

[10] De Cleyre, "Why I Am an Anarchist," Mother Earth, Vol. 3 (March 1908), pp. 20, 30.

[11] Selected Works, p. 355.

[12] De Cleyre, "They Who Marry Do Ill," pp. 501, 508-511.

[13] De Cleyre, "The Case of Woman vs. Orthodoxy," The Boston Investigator, September 19, 1896, Clipping in Labadie Collection.

[14] Margaret S. Marsh, Anarchist Women, 1870-1920 (Philadelphia: Temple University Press, 1981), p. 146.

[15] De Cleyre to Samuel H. Gordon, n.d. [1897], Joseph J. Cohen Papers, Bund Archives of the Jewish Labor Movement, New York. Much of this letter is also quoted in Avrich, American Anarchist, p. 84.

[16] Avrich, p. 161.

[17] De Cleyre, "Why I Am an Anarchist," p. 21; Selected Works, pp. 100-101, 239-240.

[18] De Cleyre to Harriet De Claire, May 27, 1907, Ishill Papers.

[19] Selected Works, p. 169.

[20] De Cleyre to Harriet De Claire, May 5, 1900, Labadie Collection. Also quoted in Blaine McKinley, "Anarchist Jeremiads: American Anarchists and American History," Journal of American Culture, Vol. 6 (Summer 1983), p. 76.

[21] Selected Works, p. 134.

[22] Selected Works, pp. 87, 90, 145.

[23] Selected Works, p. 139.

Previously unpublished quotations from Voltairine de Cleyre's letters appear with the generous permission of her granddaughter, Voltairine de Cleyre Buckwalter.

MARY CHASE PERRY STRATTON (1867 - 1961)

MARY CHASE PERRY STRATTON
ENTREPRENEURIAL ARTIST

Grace Stewart

Mary Chase Perry Stratton was both entrepreneur and artist. Although no evidence comes from direct statements made by the artist herself or by others, a tension did exist between her need to make money and her tendency to ignore that need. This tension is not uncommon among artists, but it is rare to find so evident in one person both a business drive and an artistic drive. Letters, diaries, and statements by colleagues show that those dual approaches often conflicted with one another. Ella Peters, her secretary from 1938 until 1961, remembered Stratton as both a business woman and an artist.[1]

Whether driven by the conflict between entrepreneur and artist, by her position in the family, by artistic temperament, by the spirit of her muse, or by an entrepreneurial urge, she was described by an acquaintance as a person who had to "do something."[2] Stratton herself saw the position with her siblings as an important factor in her life. In the first chapter of her unpublished autobiography, she comments on "the coolness not to say casualness" of her family's reception to her birth on March 15, 1867.[3] The chapter's title, "Born a Dau," refers to the brief note her father made of her entry into the world, whereas her brother's and sister's births were each recorded with voluminous and specific detail. This focus on her third-class citizenship occurred again in the autobiography when she wrote of having to share her siblings' sleds, inscribed with the twin names "Atlantic" and "Pacific," until she finally got her own sled with the name "Johnnie" inscribed on it. The name haunted her, supposedly, for she claimed she suffered with the nickname "Johnnie" until her father took pity and repainted the sled. Her focus on the incident with the sled brings to light not only Stratton's attention to her relations with her siblings but also her love of color, for she mentioned her disappointment that the sled was painted in slate instead of the bright green for which she had longed.[4] This early attention both to color and the desire for something to call her own remained with her throughout her life.

As a young woman, Stratton had to contend with other familial factors. Named after a friend of her mother, Mary Chase Perry was born in Hancock, Michigan. She remembered her surgeon father, William Walbridge Perry, as a man who played chess or cribbage at the local drug store with educated friends and who attended the Congregational church with the family. Stratton claimed that at an early age, her "own emotions were very much affected by religious convictions."[5] Even though she later described some of those convictions as "mis-conceptions," she remained sensitive to religious symbols.

When Stratton was only ten years old, her father was mistakenly attacked with an ax handle wielded by a man intent on punishing someone else. The following year Dr. Perry died from those injuries.[6] His wife tried to maintain the family home by renting out his office to a dentist, but eventually the family left Hancock to settle in Ann Arbor.

During this time, Stratton's skills, both entrepreneurial and artistic, were developing in several ways. Her business ventures began when she tried to help meet household financial needs while the family still lived in Hancock.

According to her autobiography, she answered an ad to sell brass lamp burners and made calls in the nearby mining community, selling burners for thirty-five cents each. The young entrepreneur explained her plan: "I hoped to save large sums of money which I could pour into my mother's lap. Instead, one of the miners confided the story of his purchase to my brother and a family council persuaded me to discontinue my trips to 'shanty town.'"[7]

Stratton's artistic endeavors developed more smoothly. Her mother's friend, Mary Chase, taught her namesake how to color, paint, and draw, and the young woman took up the popular pastime of china painting. She created flowers and leaves in soft, shadowy colors on chinaware. According to Thomas Brunk, archivist at Pewabic Pottery, Stratton "began her formal art education at the Art Academy of Cincinnati in 1887-89 with the study of design, clay modeling, and sculpting" and met in Ohio women "who were making important innovations in American ceramics."[8] In 1891, she moved to Asheville, North Carolina, where she taught china painting. She moved to Detroit in 1893 and with four other women established a studio called the Keramic Art Colony.[9]

About a year later, she became professionally involved with Horace J. Caulkins, who, with Detroit dentist Charles H. Land, had developed a kiln for firing dental work. The kiln was subsequently changed so that it could fire glazes on ceramic and glass. In 1896, Stratton began giving firing demonstrations to students and professional artists; in effect, she became a manufacturer's representative for the kiln, which was called the Revelation China Kiln.[10] Because the kiln was portable, fueled with kerosene, and easily monitored through a small hole in the door, it soon became popular with potters and ceramic artists. Its popularity may well have been connected with Stratton's sales ability or with her reputation as a china painter.[11] A contemporary described her work as "highly ornamental vases and tableware in the mode of the time--shadowy roses, lilacs, pale backgrounds and gild work, always experimenting with the effects of firing, degrees of temperatures or in the materials."[12] In any case, Stratton was busy, both with china painting and with demonstrations of the kiln, traveling in Michigan and to nearby states.

Around 1900, she became dissatisfied with what she was doing. She explained, "I had come to the point where I was restless, uneasy and not [on] any direct line leading to artistic fulfillment."[13] This restlessness suggests the existence of the tension between art and good business sense. One can imagine the debate she had with herself: if she switched her course, she might be just as restless and not as well off financially; or she might not enjoy material success but would be more fulfilled.

The passage in her autobiography dealing with this time of decision reveals her metaphysical side. She describes a stroll she took along a beach, mulling over her alternatives. As she walked along, a discarded newspaper tumbled ahead of her. Racing after it, she read an article encouraging readers to develop the resources of America. The article was "about copper and zinc and lead and clay, leading to the establishment of a clay-working school and giving possibilities and statistics."[14] According to Stratton, when she raced back to the Caulkins' cottage and asked Horace Caulkins to help her "develop the resources of the United States," he agreed without knowing what she intended.[15]

The narrative, as Stratton writes it, reveals her energy and Caulkins' support and also shows the tension between her business sense and her artistry. She was pulled by the desire to develop her artistic skills and she did so, leaving behind a relatively secure income to leap into a business about which she knew little. She was willing to risk, a trait needed by a true entrepreneur. Fortunately, she had Caulkins' backing.

In 1901, Caulkins and Stratton rented a carriage house or stable on John R and Alfred in Detroit, where they began experimenting. Perry and Caulkins hired Joseph Herrick, an Alsatian potter, to throw the shapes Stratton drew in outline and also hired a young boy, Julius Albus, to help her while she experimented with colors for glazes—shimmering coppers, reds, blues, and greens. To learn the business, Stratton visited major art potteries and, in 1901 and 1902, studied ceramics under Charles F. Binns at Alfred University in New York state.

Stratton's new pottery company produced primarily vases in the Art Nouveau style. Then an order came from Frederick Stearns Company for containers to hold cold cream. Perry submitted several designs, and the company chose a four-sided jar with a medium blue glaze. Initially seen as a boon, the order became a nightmare. The small jars could not be thrown on the wheel. Due to uneven shrinkage in covers and jars, the aftermath of the firing, according to Perry, became

> a fitting contest—a row of jars on the table, a cover in hand passed quickly along, tapping, tapping until it fitted a jar. How many dozens—gross—we would fit in this way for hours at a time, Mr Caulkins taking his part with Julius and me...As wonderful as it seemed at first, the difficulty in fitting covers proved the fly in the ointment, and after about a year, [we] gave it up as not being the most direct road to achieving an art product.[17]

In addition, Ella Peters points out that, since the covers were not airtight, the cold cream soon dried out.[18] Stratton the entrepreneur had to weigh the amount of effort, the income, and the achievement of art. The cosmetic jar project ceased. Stratton continued to experiment in glazes and shapes, however, going for advice to the owner of Burley's Stores in Chicago, and coming home with a carte blanche order for $1000 worth of bowls and lamp jars. When Burley asked for a trade name, she submitted several, and in 1903 he chose "Pewabic" for its Indian and American flavor. Later, Stratton discovered that the word meant "clay with a copper color." She claimed that the title "Pewabic Pottery" appealed to her "as being rather 'spooky' and foreordained."[19] Her mystical side was showing again.

Stratton's business side was evident in her approach to clay tiles. Lacking the equipment normally used to manufacture tiles, she nevertheless ventured to develop them by hand and discovered that architects preferred the handmade tiles, ordering them for fireplace surrounds, fountains, and countertops. It was these beautiful clay tiles that eventually gave Mary Chase Perry Stratton the financial success she was seeking and it is for these architectural embellishments that she is most remembered. To accommodate the increase in business, she and Caulkins looked for property on which to build a more suitable plant. That she was truly an entrepreneurial artist is most evident in her description of what the new building meant to her:

> It was a fulfillment of an ideal, justified by the material success of finding a market for our productions. In any art coupled with manufacture, an arbitrary decree pronounces the product as good or bad in direct ratio to the public demand, regardless of artistic merit. On this ground...I could not help feeling a warm satisfaction over what we had been able to accomplish.[20]

Caulkins and Perry chose a friend, William Buck Stratton, as the architect for the new building, a Tudor two-story edifice with a Kentish-inn look, which was erected on Jefferson Avenue in 1907.

The new building brought with its construction a new relationship. As the potter explained:

> In connection with the many conferences which were a necessary part of the perfect understanding between architect and client, something more than that grew up between William Stratton and me. I found myself dependent on his point of view in many ways. He appreciated and understood the position in which I had placed myself, almost mortgaging my future to the development of the Pottery.[21]

But the relationship did not bloom fully, given the time constraints on both artist entrepreneur and architect. As Stratton explained, "We were each individually busy with family demands which it took almost one hundred percent of free time to fulfill."[22]

While the pottery was growing, so was the arts and craft movement in Detroit. Mary Chase Perry Stratton, Caulkins, and William Stratton helped in 1906 to found the Detroit Society of Arts and Crafts (later to become the Center for Creative Studies) and served as trustees of the Detroit Museum of Art. The Pewabic Pottery itself was a part of the movement. As Thomas Brunk points out, "Pewabic Pottery was the most significant manifestation of the International Arts and Crafts movement in ceramics in Michigan."[23] But even this artistic milieu was perceived with an entrepreneurial eye by Stratton, the potter. The Society of Arts and Crafts provided an opportunity for display of her pottery and the artistic milieu stimulated her development. As she said, "Naturally, the Society and Pewabic Pottery benefitted mutually from these contacts. Through the National Federation of Arts, our vases were shown at centers throughout the country. We also sent objects to the Paris exposition where they received high honor."[24]

Although proud of the success of the pottery, Stratton had to make difficult choices in order to maintain standards of art. After Burley died, buyers from his store demanded products based solely on their sales prospects. The artist wrote:

> It was not easy at the peak of a profitable line to make up our minds to give it up. That is exactly what we did do, taking a stand once for all, that our product, in pottery at least, should express our own judgment and artistic taste. Otherwise, there was no fun about our adventure, and most of all, even though we were hoping to make ends meet, we wanted to work with real pleasure and satisfaction. What is there in making a thousand pin-trays, if they have not your sound and sincere approval, even though they make a profit for you? I realize this sort of reasoning is not consistent with the usual business man's views.[25]

Fortunately, Caulkins was willing to follow her lead and to give up the profits. Stratton says, "It was purely a spiritual valuation that stopped up a channel of distribution in order to permit an unknown objective to flower into something in advance of what we had done."[26] In 1913, production of lamps and shades was discontinued.[27]

Prior to this cessation and prodded by the Detroit art collector, Charles L. Freer, Stratton had produced six iridescent glazes, working on the formulae between 1906 and 1909 until the glazes could be reproduced at will. The effects were not always entirely satisfactory to her, but with each experiment, vases fired with the new glazes became more

Mary Chase Perry Stratton

appealing to art collectors and architects. They began ordering these remarkable ceramics with their brilliant colors and flashes of fire. Consequently, ceasing the production of lamps and shades for Burley's was not quite the risky business suggested by Stratton's autobiographical sketch, since she was already making glazes which would eventually produce even better money-makers. As Stratton explained:

> Vases of this nature soon gained popularity, and possibly many people feel that it is the most typical effect of Pewabic. Personally it has a strong appeal to me when the surface is not too brilliant, and changing lights seem to come and go, yet show a depth which the eye ever seeks to penetrate.[28]

To develop these glazes, Stratton had to experiment constantly, noting each change, each variable, and finally recording the outcome in her formula book. Describing the work done, Mrs. Nebe wrote:

> Mr. Caulkins had made a study of the gases and heats and Mary Chase of clays and mixtures and chemicals, and sometimes of physical geography, to determine what adulterant might have been part of some elusive glaze effect....She worked for years to get and perfect the wonderful blue--Egyptian blue--that we see in the museums. To the artistic sense has been added hard, hard work.[29]

The hard work was rewarded. Architects began to requested the pottery--glazed and unglazed--for homes, buildings, museums, and churches. The buildings which contained these shimmering blue and green Pewabic tiles include the Detroit Institute of Arts, Christ Church Cranbrook, Cathedral

Church of St. Paul, the Guardian Building, Meadowbrook, St. Aloysius, the Shrine of the Immaculate Conception in Washington, D.C., and numerous private homes in Grosse Pointe and Detroit.

In the early days of that success, William Stratton designed a home for the potter at 138 East Grand Boulevard in Detroit. On June 19, 1918, when she was 51, they married at the home of Horace J. Caulkins, and moved into the East Grand Boulevard home. There they lived until 1928, when they dismantled the house and used the materials to build a more elaborate home on Three Mile Drive in Grosse Pointe Park, a mutual venture designed by her architect husband and filled with her pottery. Their marriage was a forerunner of the modern dual-career family, two people building careers and eventually combining households. But Stratton's early descriptions of her architect friend reveal their attraction towards one another. According to Lillian Myers Pear, "There was an unusual bond between them; he strengthened her profession and knowledge of architecture, and greatly enriched her life."[30] But shortly after the Strattons had built the beautiful new home, the Great Depression struck. The number of tile installations declined and they were forced to sell their home and to move into more modest surroundings in to keep the pottery and its potters working. The conflict between art and business took its toll.

At the height of success, when a group of women came to the Pottery to view the works, Mary Chase Stratton and Caulkins purposely removed the price tags, hoping that each vase might be judged on its own merits and that each person would evaluate it strictly on its aesthetic appeal. The group was not content, however, until some price had been set on the pieces. Stratton wrote, "This experience brought home to me that we are not yet on a plane of adjudicating spiritual values without knowledge of material worth."[31] Her impatience with that need to set a monetary value on a work of art was evident again when she described her work for the fountain in the Seiberling residence. For this design, she took a creative clue from Wordsworth's description of the wedding party at St. Kean's well. The myth decreed that whoever succeeded in drinking first from the well would rule the household. With this conceptual framework, Stratton was eager to begin working on the fountain instead of estimating costs. She wanted Renaissance patrons like the DeMedici and complained:

> Do we suppose that the artists of that golden period would ever have brought forth their masterpieces, if they had been obliged to make an estimate beforehand? Why shouldn't the President of the United States or even rubber magnates say in a loud voice, "Your idea is good--start in--mix your clay--fire it in the kiln, whatever the cost is, we will meet it.[32]

The entrepreneur and the artist were continually at odds. Ella Peters claims that, when she began working for Stratton, there was no accurate cost accounting, so that sometimes the pottery would operate at a loss on a particular job. Peters devised a system which charged the hours worked to a specific project. Nevertheless, when Stratton undertook tiling a pieta for a church in Toledo, Peters advised her that they were going over the budget and the potter still ordered the work to continue because she liked doing it and the church had no more money.[33]

Despite this seeming nonchalance about finances, Stratton's entrepreneurial bent can still be seen in business letters such as the correspondence with George Booth concerning an installation at Cranbrook.[34] Supposedly miffed by a reduction of a large order, Stratton indicated that she was not interested in doing the job at all. Thomas Brunk believed that the incident stemmed from Mrs. Stratton's loyalty to the Detroit Arts and Crafts Society and her feeling that Booth was pulling away from that group, favoring outside artists, and unwilling to pay for the quality of Pewabic tile.[35] The incident speaks both to Stratton's artistic sense and to her desire for the income coming from the larger order.

In many cases, the need to keep the pottery going was paramount. Without continuing business, the pottery would have been forced to close during the depression. Even after William Stratton died in 1938 when his wife was 71, she continued to operate the plant. That the potters continued to work speaks to both her entrepreneurial abilities and her artistic sensibility.

That sensibility was evident until her death. When Stratton was in her 90's, her secretary, Ellen Peters, heard smashing of pottery. She moved toward the sound and found Stratton destroying her early pieces of china painting, which she no longer thought worthy of display. Peters convinced Stratton to desist for the moment and thereby saved the rest of the collection.[36]

Having received acclaim, including an honorary degree from the University of Michigan and the Charles Fergus Binns Medal for contribution to the ceramic industry, Mary Chase Perry Stratton might also have considered selling her famous formula to gain a fortune. Instead, she worried about its falling into hands lacking artistic sensibility. She confided this worry to Mrs. Peters, who promised that the formula would never be passed along.[37] Mrs. Stratton died on April 15, 1961, without revealing the formula, but leaving a pottery and an artistic legacy that continued beyond her death. She was clear about that legacy:

One never learns anything by copying others, but by constant experiments, one can arrive at something which is distinctly his own. Artists do not stand in reflected glow. They may borrow ideas, but great ones give something of themselves to creative art that no one else has given.[38]

Mary Chase Perry Stratton showed us what was possible when an entrepreneurial spirit is combined with an artistic sensibility. Thanks to renovation by the Pewabic Society, the Pewabic Pottery continues to produce fine pieces on the original site, which has been placed on the National Register of Historic Places. Mary Chase Stratton well deserves the honor she received by being admitted into the Michigan Women's Hall of Fame in 1986. She was, indeed, both an entrepreneur and an artist.

NOTES

[1] Ella Peters, personal interview, April 30, 1987, Detroit, Michigan.

[2] Letter from Mrs. Albert J. Nebe to Louise Orth, October 13, 1932.

[3] Mary Chase Perry Stratton, "Adventures in Ceramics," unpublished typescript, p.1.

[4] Stratton, p.4.

[5] Stratton, p.5.

[6] Stratton, p. 11.

[7] Stratton, p. 11.

[8] Thomas W. Brunk, "Ceramics in Michigan, 1886-1906," The Arts and Crafts Movement in Michigan: 1887-1906 (Detroit: Pewabic Society, 1986), p. 24.

[9] Brunk, p. 24.

[10] Brunk, p. 25.

[11] Brunk, p. 25.

[12] Nebe, letter.
[13] Stratton, p. 24.
[14] Stratton, p. 25.
[15] Stratton, p. 26.
[16] Brunk, p. 26.
[17] Stratton, p. 40.
[18] Peters, interview.
[19] Stratton, p. 48.
[20] Stratton, p. 56.
[21] Stratton, p. 60.
[22] Stratton, p. 60.
[23] Brunk, p. 28.
[24] Stratton, p. 54.
[25] Stratton, p. 67.
[26] Stratton, p. 67.
[27] Brunk, p. 28.
[28] Perry, p. 72.
[29] Nebe, letter.
[30] Lillian Myers Pear, The Pewabic Pottery (Des Moines, Iowa: Wallace, Homestead, 1976). p. 81
[31] Stratton, p. 75.
[32] Stratton, p. 99.
[33] Peters, interview.
[34] Letters from George G. Booth dated October 16 and 21, 1918.
[35] Brunk, telephone interview, May 16, 1987.
[36] Peters, interview.
[37] Peters, interview.
[38] Pear, p. 261.

MARTHA LONGSTREET (1870 – 1953)

MARTHA LONGSTREET
CHILDREN'S DOCTOR

Evelyn Shields

Martha Longstreet decided to become a physician "because no other profession offers such opportunities for service."[1] This philosophy, carried out in her life work, placed her among the leading citizens in her community and in the state. At her death, a newspaper article stated that "she has taken her rightful place among the giants--the illustrious of Saginaw and Michigan history."[2]

Longstreet was born April 27, 1870 in Erie, Pennsylvania, but moved to Unionville, Michigan as a young girl. She came to Saginaw in 1887 to train as a nurse at Bliss Deaconess Hospital, operated by the Methodist Council. It later merged with Saginaw General Hospital. After graduation, she worked as a private duty nurse for six years. Because of her ability and zeal for the job, she came to the attention of the hospital staff doctors who encouraged her to study medicine. In 1904 Martha Longstreet graduated with honors from the University of Illinois Medical School, one of only 19 women in a class of 200 men. Later she did postgraduate work at Harvard University and at Post Graduate Hospital in New York City.

Upon returning to Saginaw, Dr. Longstreet opened a medical practice at 520 Hayden, the lifelong home she shared with her brother across from the old Saginaw High School.[3]

She worked out of this office for 45 years, 28 of them spent in the practice of pediatrics. In 1905 she became attending physician at Children's Home and at the Home for the Aged. At the age of 78, Dr. Longstreet retired due to failing eyesight. She died February 26, 1953.

These statistics on Martha Longstreet give only the skeleton of this remarkable lady's life; they do not begin to flesh out the real person. The Martha Longstreet who became the most remarkable woman in Saginaw County history cannot be deciphered by statistics alone.

Dr. Longstreet was not the first female doctor in Saginaw. As early as 1874, a Dr. Evans had opened a practice. She was later followed by other women, two of whom were on the faculty of Saginaw Valley Medical College in the 1880's.[4]

There were several factors which motivated a woman to study medicine at that time. For one thing, state medical schools were becoming coeducational. There were, and still are, advantages to entering the medical profession. A physician could practice as long as health permitted and patients had confidence in her. Retirement due to age was not a necessity. A doctor could be her own boss. She dealt with all ages and with all individuals. She was accorded social status as a member of a learned profession. Friendships were developed through membership in various medical and lay organizations. And perhaps most important of all, for Martha Longstreet was the satisfaction of relieving suffering and saving lives.

Many people at that time, however, were opposed to female doctors on the basis of sex. An often-heard argument was that the study of medicine would make a woman coarse and unfeminine, so discrimination often had to be reckoned with.[5] It is, therefore, significant that Dr. Longstreet's long years of service did much to enhance the standing of women doctors here and elsewhere. She was never resented by the male doctors, but earned their respect through her professional ability. This acceptance was unusual, but she was an unusual person.

As a young woman, Martha Longstreet's health was almost broken in her nursing career. At that time, the job consisted of all types of manual labor. Nurses were expected to scrub floors and do laundry as well as to care for patients. Despite suffering from a spinal curvature which nagged with pain and drained her physical strength, she was not deterred from studying medicine.

Longstreet began the life of a general practitioner in the early days of this century. Even though she had an office, the average person had no way of getting to it. It was the doctor's responsibility to visit the patient. Try to picture this woman doctor going from house to house, in all kinds of weather, day and night, to visit sick and dying patients. Imagine her typical day: rushing from an emergency delivery of a premature baby to assist the surgeon operating on a ruptured appendix, keeping crowded office hours that are held up by a sudden death, driving miles to make house calls, and sitting through the night by a crib of a baby suffering with pneumonia.

Dr. Longstreet was on the consulting staffs of St. Luke's, St. Mary's and Saginaw General hospitals, and was known as an expert diagnostician. In 1921, when she decided to limit her practice to children, she wanted to be known as a children's doctor and not as a pediatrician. "There is something about taking care of children. When they look up into your eyes and smile that honest kind of smile, it gives you something money can't buy."[6] As a children's doctor, she delivered thousands of Saginawians and preserved the lives of many more.

For years Dr. Longstreet had a practice so heavy it was almost more than she could handle. She worked day and night but was never too tired to respond to a call. She was the only staff doctor at Children's Hospital, sometimes fighting epidemics almost alone. The Saginaw News remembers that she "began making her visits driving her own horse through the mud before we had a pavement, climbing stairs before we owned an elevator, and working singlehanded against all limitations of the times to give children all she had to give to any hour of the day or night."[7] She worked around the clock during the influenza epidemic of 1918, saving many lives that would otherwise have been lost.

No matter where she went, "whether it was to the small houses huddled by the railroad tracks or in sections where housemaids answered the door, her appearance was an event."[8] Three generations of people believed that no matter how grave the situation, things were not so bad when she came. She earned the love and respect of the entire community, not only through her professional abilities but also because of her personal concern for the families she helped. Once when she called to help deliver a child, she found the husband had gone to work leaving a houseful of small children. After delivering the baby, she fed and bathed the other children before putting them to bed.[9]

Her medical billing was unusual. Rates were based on such concerns as how long it took the family provider to get back to work or whether a large family could afford to pay doctor bills. She would notice the lack of food on the table or the threadbare rug; food and clothing often mysteriously arrived after Dr. Martha Longstreet finished a case.

She charged $2.50 for her first delivery and the grateful mother named her baby daughter "Martha Longstreet."[10] Everyone attests to the special way she had with children. She knew how to address their interests and always carried gum and candy in her bag. Gertrude Hamlin remembers dramatically her childhood encounter with Martha Longstreet.

I was very ill with the flu in 1918 and Dr. Longstreet would come to the house and stay there all night sometimes, because I was unconscious part of the time. When she got me out of the worst part of it she told me, "Now if you will try to eat this ice cream when I ask you to, I'm going to see that you have something you want very much." So I, of course, tried desperately to eat the ice cream. I did eat it. Then she went out of the room; I could hear her skirts rustling. When she came back, she had this great big thing with a sheet over it and came over and said, "Now do you think you can pull that sheet off?" Well, I guess I tried but she had to help me because I was too weak. She took it off and there was my doll with the head all fixed. You see, it had been broken and she bought this lovely head with the curly hair and I was so happy...I was about nine years old then.[11]

Longstreet was so beloved that children continued seeing her beyond the age when they needed a pediatrician. Patricia Riddick, who took her nurses training at Saginaw General Hospital, remembers Dr. Longstreet's remarkable presence in the operating room. When babies would contract pyloric stenosis (a navel infection), they needed an immediate operation. "Because she was not a surgeon, Dr. Powers did the surgery for her. I used to scrub in the operating room. The anesthesia for the baby was an ounce of whiskey with sugar in it. While the doctor was making the incision to release the spasm, Dr. Longstreet would stand in the operating room chatting away to that month-old baby. She was a soothing person to have around. She bolstered everybody."[12]

Besides being an outstanding physician, Martha Longstreet was a person whose philosophy of life was shaped by experience. In piecing together a composite picture of this woman, what emerges is a person who had a clear idea of her values, her priorities, and her destiny. There is little doubt that she loved what she did and was guided by an inherent idealism. Although she never married, there were no regrets on her part. Her life was so full she could not have done justice to all the people she helped if family responsibilities had interferred.

Martha Longstreet did not look her height because of a marked spinal curvature. Without the physical handicap, she would have been about five feet seven inches tall. Her trademarks were the gaily flowered hats she wore everywhere; some say they served to divert sick children during examinations. Her dresses, usually in her favorite color of blue, were covered with ribbons and lace as a means of taking attention away from her deformity. She always wore her dresses long, even after it was unfashionable to do so. In the office, she wore a white coat, but it was always open so you could see her dress. One observer recalled that she looked like somebody's grandmother.[13]

"When she came in the corridors of the hospital, it was just like a ray of sunshine coming in. She had a deep, hearty voice and always greeted you with a 'well, how are we doing today.' in a very positive and lively style."[14] When she assured the child "everything's going to be all right," he never doubted it.

Dr. Longstreet was a sincere, sympathetic person well liked by her colleagues. Even though she was independent, "she was always loving, not haughty, not disdainful. She wanted your love and gave love in return."[15]

A good converstionalist, she could talk recipes or politics, and her wit was well known. Once a man sympathized with her for having to come out on such a cold night. "You should have a husband to take you out at night and show you a good time," he said. Knowing the man's wife took in washing and seeing the racks of wet clothes the woman had just finished before being overcome with labor pains, Longstreet replied, "Did you ever hear of an old maid taking in washing?"[16]

Despite the fact that she had one of the largest medical practices in Saginaw, Dr. Longstreet still found time to devote to civic groups. She liked people and was active in clubs, social work, and church groups.

In 1912 efforts were begun to centralize Saginaw's charitable work. Because of her continuing interest in social welfare and work with charitable organizations, Dr. Longstreet was the motivating force which helped to coordinate Saginaw's social service groups into the Council of Social Agencies. She was also on the original committee which established the Visiting Nurses Association in Saginaw County.

Dr. Longstreet's community service was outstanding. She served on the consulting staffs of three hospitals and was a member of the County Medical Society and the Michigan Medical Association. In addition, she served on the Board of Directors of the First Ward Community Center, and her leadership was a factor which helped the Center grow and become one of Saginaw's outstanding community enterprises. She was instrumental in setting up and equipping the Center's clinic for preschool children where vaccinations and immunizations against whooping cough and diphtheria were given. In 13 years she missed only one Board meeting of the organization.[17]

She was director of the Saginaw Community Chest and later was made an honorary member. For many years, Dr. Longstreet also served on the Board of the City Rescue Mission, was active in raising funds for the YWCA, was a member of the Saginaw American Association of University Women, and the Saginaw Chapter of the DAR. She was a charter member of the Saginaw Business and Professional

Women's Association. This organization considered her its most distinguished member because of her standing in the community and her years of self-sacrificing work performed quietly and unassumingly.

Although later in life she minimized all the "fuss" people made about her, Martha Longstreet became a legend in her own time. She was recognized, feted, and paid tribute to by every sector in the community. Beginning in 1937 and continuing long after her death, the honors accorded this woman were impressive. When the Children's Home opened its new nursery in 1937, it was called the Martha Longstreet Nursery in dedication to the lady who ministered to its residents for so many years.

A year later the Michigan Women's Clubs and Associations designated her Michigan's most outstanding woman. The tribute said she was honored for her achievements "because the success or failure of every woman in business or the professions reflects upon the entire sex and...a woman who achieves success in any one field...makes it considerably easier for those of us who follow her."[18]

In 1940 Martha Longstreet was honored at a testimonial dinner in Detroit and presented with life membership by the Michigan branch of the American Women's Medical Association. That same year the Saginaw Chamber of Commerce elected her an honorary member of its Board of Directors and named her to receive Saginaw's highest civic award—Saginaw's 1940 Outstanding Citizen of the Year Award.[19] She was the first woman recipient of this award.

One of the finest tributes paid her was the Saginaw County Medical Society testimonial dinner in her honor when she was praised as one "whose lifetime of devotion, unselfish service and untiring activity in the realm of medicine has earned for her the distinction of being one of the first and foremost pediatricians in Michigan."[20]

The following year, Dr. Longstreet was made a life member of St. Luke's Senior Medical Staff because as hospital board president Erwin J. Geyer said, "in your daily life you are an exemplification of the highest respect and regard for the medical profession."[21] The Saginaw District Nurses Association also made her a honorary member.

Later she received the Aerie's Civic Award given by the Eagles Auxiliary of the Eagles Home, was honored by Zonta and Quota Clubs, and named life member of the Michigan State Medical Society and the Saginaw Business and Professional Women's Association. When Martha Longstreet officially retired as active director of the First Ward Community Center in 1949, the children's clinic which she helped to establish was named the Dr. Martha Longstreet Clinic.

In 1953, shortly after her death, the Saginaw School Board decided to name a new elementary school in her honor as a fitting tribute and recognition of her many years of service as Saginaw's doctor for children. At the school's dedication, a Saginaw News editor wrote: "Suffice it to say few Saginawians in recent generations have so richly deserved to have a school named in their honor, and Dr. Longstreet, if she were here today, could wish no greater honor."[22] Her portrait still hangs in the school.

Martha Longstreet was one of five charter members in the Saginaw Hall of Fame and remains one of only five women inducted up to the present time. She was admitted to the Michigan Women's Hall of Fame in 1984.

In 1977, Saginaw General Hospital Auxiliary hung her portrait in the hospital's main lobby in recognition of her leadership which contributed to the growth of the hospital.

We can justify these honors as being significant in assessing this woman's contribution to the betterment of society. There is a remarkable consistency to the recognition given her. It is, without exception, generous and enthusiastic. There is no evidence of rancor or jealousy. Rarely does one find such general acclamation for one individual. Martha Longstreet stories and legends abound, many of them connected with her psychological intuition and her charitable billing; they are all based on fact. This service to others won her respect and love. And her honors are evidence of that love and of the esteem in which the community held her. Dr. Martha Longstreet was the most famous and revered woman of her time in Saginaw County history.

She never sought praise or notoriety but won widespread recognition in a career as one of the state's foremost pediatricians. Her impeccable professional ethics also won her widespread admiration and her advice was often sought by respectful male colleagues.

Martha Longstreet was more than an outstanding physician. She was a human being to whom patients were not mere cases, but people consumed with fear and worry. Because she was aware of this, she administered kindness along with the medicine. The Saginaw News editorialized that this kindness "built in the hearts of all who knew her a memorial which will endure as long as memory itself endures."[23]

Tributes like "No other man or woman in this community has given so much to so many" and "Saginaw could not have been Saginaw without her" and "this community has been enriched by the beauty of your life" abound.[24] At a testimonial dinner, she was given a volume of letters as the only gift she would not give away to the first needy family. As a result of her lifelong generosity, she left no estate. Her legacy was what she had given of herself in life. To Dr. Longstreet, the best reward in practicing medicine was not fame or fortune but the opportunity to render human service.

Today, women have entered every profession, but in 1904 when Martha Longstreet began to practice medicine, women

Martha Longstreet

doctors were rare and the public lacked confidence in the ability of women to succeed as physicians. She overcame this prejudice and established herself as a leader in her field. Dr. Martha Longstreet proved that not only was she an outstanding practitioner, but that she was personally suited to the demands of the profession despite a physical handicap. She left as her legacy an exemplary life which stands as an inspiration for all women.

NOTES

[1] The Saginaw News, April 10, 1938.
[2] The Saginaw News, April 10, 1938.
[3] Inteview with Richard D. Mudd, M.D., March 1, 1987.
[4] Anita M. Fisk, The History of Saginaw County Medicine, (Midland, Michigan: Pendell Publishing, Inc., 1986), pp. 9, 49.
[5] Bertha Van Hoosen, Petticoat Surgeon, (Chicago: People's Book Club, 1947), p. 213.
[6] The Saginaw News, October 1, 1937.
[7] The Saginaw News, October, 1, 1937.
[8] The Saginaw News, December 29, 1968.
[9] The Saginaw News, January 25, 1970.
[10] The Saginaw News, September 3, 1964.
[11] Interview with Gertrude Hamlin, January 23, 1987.
[12] Interview with Patricia Riddick, January 23, 1987.
[13] Riddick interview.
[14] Riddick interview.
[15] Riddick interview.
[16] The Saginaw News, January 25, 1970.
[17] The Saginaw News, July 6, 1949.
[18] The Saginaw News, April 10, 1938.
[19] Minutes of the Board of Directors Meeting, December 10, 1940, Saginaw Chamber of Commerce, Saginaw, Michigan (in the files of the Chamber).

Historic Women of Michigan

[20] Saginaw County Medical Society, <u>Testimonial Dinner Honoring Dr. Martha Longstreet</u>, December 10, 1946.
[21] <u>The Saginaw News</u>, October 29, 1947.
[22] <u>The Saginaw News</u>, July 16, 1953.
[23] <u>The Saginaw News</u>, February 27, 1953.
[24] <u>The Saginaw News</u>, December 11, 1946.

MARY CARMELITA MANNING, R.S.M. (1888-1962)

MARY CARMELITA MANNING, R.S.M., FOUNDER OF MERCY COLLEGE OF DETROIT

Susan Bakke

Mary Carmelita Manning, R.S.M., was a modern pioneer. Her vision, social commitment, and civic endeavors contributed significantly to developing Michigan's present systems of health care, education, and social services. Affectionately known as "Mother Carmelita" within her religious community and by others who knew her well, she always remained first and foremost a dedicated Sister of Mercy.[1] It was from the tradition of the order's founder, Mother Catherine McAuley, that Mary Carmelita Manning found the work which nourished her heart, and from doing the work which nourished her own heart, she served others. Her natural talents for business, unusual for a woman in her time and of her vocational choice, quickly placed her in leadership positions both within her order and in a broader social context. The source of her power as a leader flowed from her unusual personality. She combined compassion for others with an uncanny organizational and business sense. This combination enabled her to transform her desire to improve health care for the sick and poor into actuality. Mother Carmelita identified the needs of each community which she served, formulated workable solutions, and then produced dramatic results. She committed herself fully to each task undertaken, following the path which balanced her mind and her heart.

As a Religious Sister of Mercy, Mother Carmelita served humanity selflessly for fifty-three years.[2] During this time she founded many hospitals and schools, including Mercy College of Detroit, and participated in numerous health and community organizations. Her influence remains in every community where she worked. The hospitals and schools she founded continue to embody her dedication to the service of humankind.

Born Mary S. Manning on December 24, 1888, in Lansing, Iowa, to Jeremiah and Kate Dungan Manning, Mother Carmelita was one of nine children.[3] When she was still very young, her family moved from Iowa to South Dakota. Along with her brothers and sisters, she was educated in the public schools of Bereford, South Dakota. Even as a young woman, she felt drawn toward serving others. In 1908 she entered a three-year nursing program at St. Joseph Mercy Hospital in Dubuque, Iowa. During her nurse's training, she became deeply influenced by the Religious Sisters of Mercy and decided to follow a religious vocation. On February 2, 1909, she entered the novitiate of the Dubuque Mercy Community. Later, she completed her nursing degree while simultaneously pursuing her religious studies. On September 24, 1911, she made her perpetual vows, and Mary S. Manning became Mary Carmelita Manning, R.S.M.[4]

The newly professed sister's first assignment was to St. Joseph Mercy Hospital in Ann Arbor, Michigan. From 1911 to 1922, she served as a dedicated and compassionate nurse, tending the physical and spiritual needs of all her patients, regardless of their color, religion, or economic status. From 1922 to 1927, she served as an administrator, beginning to use talents important to her future work. It was in Ann Arbor that she realized an unmet need for medical care and social services to the poor. Her colleagues were quick to recognize her organizational ability and they continued to increase her administrative responsibilities.[5]

Once given the opportunity to apply her "astute business sense" and her "constructive wizardry," she immediately began to focus her energy on health-related projects across the state of Michigan.[6] Her drive and determination were boundless as she not only improved the efficiency of her own hospital, but also assisted in constructing three other major hospitals during the same time period. Those projects included an addition to Detroit's St. Joseph Mercy Hospital in 1923, the construction of Ann Arbor's Mercywood Sanitarium in 1924, and the building of Pontiac's St. Joseph Mercy Hospital in 1927.[7] Her first years as an hospital administrator gave Mother Carmelita practical experience in finance, engineering, politics, and management, enabling her to connect her compassionate insights with effective social action. These experiences strengthened her natural aptitude for planning and inspired her to fulfill her dream of providing quality education and health care for everyone. It was at that juncture that her vision of improved social care and her talent for creating and directing new facilities began to coalesce into a formidable plan which would sweep two Mercy Provinces and encompass six states.

Responding to her talent for leadership, the order elected her as Assistant Mother Superior of the Dubuque Mercy Community.[8] "Mother Carmelita" became her official title, and her task expanded to working with other Catholic leaders to direct and shape the future missions of the Religious Sisters of Mercy. An openness to others and a powerful response to their needs became the hallmark of her leadership style.

After her term as Assistant Mother Superior came to an end in 1929, she enrolled in Marygrove College of Detroit, Michigan, to earn a Bachelor of Arts Degree, which she completed in 1930.[9] Her own experience convinced her that "a good liberal arts education was the best foundation out of which young people might choose a career."[10] She insisted that the novices in her order be liberally educated and that liberal education be at the core of all the schools she founded. When she established Mercy College of Detroit in 1941, she stood her ground against Archbishop Edward Mooney's proposal that the institution concern itself exclusively with the training of nurses. She insisted on a four-year liberal arts college.[11] Mercy College developed and grew out of the creative tension between these opposing views, with a curriculum which balances liberal arts education and professional training.

Between 1930 and 1932, Mother Carmelita served as Mother Superior and Administrator of St. Joseph Mercy Hospital in Pontiac, Michigan, the same hospital she had helped to found three years earlier. She worked tirelessly to fulfill many roles, including some from which women were generally excluded at the time. She never shirked from extending herself in areas where her efforts would benefit the poor, the sick, or the troubled.[12]

After the amalgamation of the many congregations of the Sisters of Mercy into a union, Mother Carmelita was elected Assistant Administrator of the Mercy Cincinnati Province in 1932. In 1936, she was elected Mother Provincial, holding that office until 1940. With the position of Mother Superior came increased responsibility but also the power to initiate and carry out her own visionary projects. Mother Carmelita continued to travel among her province's six states: Michigan, Indiana, Iowa, Ohio, Kentucky, and Tennessee.[13] She visited the various groups of Sisters, often entertaining them with her humorous storytelling. At the same time, she directed the planning, fundraising, designing, and building of projects which were often hundreds of miles apart. From 1937 to 1940, she guided the founding and building of the

Cincinnati Provincialate while simultaneously overseeing the construction of Mt. Carmel Mercy Hospital in Detroit in 1938. She supervised each project from inception to completion with unusual personal involvement.

Mother Carmelita was very proud of Mt. Carmel, considering it her own response to Detroit's need to care for the impoverished. It was she who turned the first spade of earth for the foundation, and she who climbed the girders during its construction to inspect the workmanship.[14] Some said that Mother Carmelita knew as much about engineering as any trained engineer and that reading blueprints was "like a piece of cake" for her.[15] Her experience and ability opened doors to the male-dominated business world of the 1940s and 1950s, and the men she worked with respected her knowledge and reliability.[16] She bridged the sheltered world of the nun and the more open world of business, transforming systems of health care and education with her spiritual values and Christian humanism.

1940 brought about great change for both the Cincinnati Sisters of Mercy and Mother Carmelita. The province voted to divide and form a new Detroit province. Mother Carmelita was appointed the first Mother Provincial of the new province. In this capacity, she was charged with founding the new provincial community and identifying its missions. She left behind her beloved Cincinnati community and embarked on an unknown adventure, commandeering an empty floor in St. Joseph Mercy Hospital in Ann Arbor as a temporary place for the sisters to work and live.[17] She then searched the city of Detroit for a suitable spot to build a women's college which would be based on the religious philosophy of the order.

During one excursion to scout the terrain, she noticed a large empty lot with a "for sale" sign nailed to an ancient tree. The land was located at West Outer Drive and Southfield. She asked her driver to stop the car, got out, looked around, pulled the sign off the tree, and immediately directed him to the address on the sign. She then marched into the real estate office and deposited twenty-five dollars as a down-payment on her dream. Within a matter of a few years, the empty lot with the ancient tree became a substantial and well-respected nursing and liberal arts college.[18] Between 1940 and 1941 Mother Carmelita designed, funded, organized, and opened Mercy College of Detroit. During the initial years, the five-story administration building, which still stands in that capacity, served as living quarters for the nuns, offices for the administration and faculty, and classrooms for the students. Shortly after the building was completed, the United States entered World War II, hindering the further development of the college. For the next four years, "priorities, lack of manpower, and the unavailability of materials were all against her, but to her, obstacles were incentives."[19] She continued her work on the Detroit Mercy provincialate and novate buildings, as well as nurturing and strengthening the fledgling college.

Of all her accomplishments, Mother Carmelita was perhaps proudest of Mercy College of Detroit, because it enabled the nuns to transmit the Mercy philosophy to the women of Michigan. She believed that there were no vocations more important than the three merciful works of nursing, teaching, and social work.[20] Consequently, these three professions became the core of Mercy College's curriculum. To this day, the College remains faithful to her vision of a strong study of the liberal arts, interwoven with the practical application of professional study. In her own words she described the qualities which she wished the college experience to instill in the students:

> You must have a keen appreciation of ethical and humanitarian ideals. You must have skill in

coordinating the activities of persons and groups performing a variety of tasks at different levels of responsibility. The basis of this principle is that it represents not only human values, but also an indispensible motive in directing your efforts and responsibilities for the common welfare.[21]

Mercy College of Detroit grew to personify Mother Carmelita's diverse commitment to the broad spectrum of human service. One of its pioneering moves was the addition of substance abuse education into its curriculum. Because of her concern and efforts, many of her hospitals were among the first to incorporate substance abuse clinics into their services.

In 1941 Mother Carmelita was presented with her first award, the Tri-State Assembly Key for distinguished service in the health and hospital fields. She was again honored in 1942, this time as the recipient of the Distinguished Service Cross of The National Catholic Hospital Association. Archbishop Stritch presented her with the cross and praised her "outstanding contribution to the fields of Catholic education, hospital administration, and community organization."[22] She accepted these awards in the same spirit with which she would receive all future awards, "not as a tribute to herself, but to the Sisters of Mercy of whom she was a deeply spiritual exemplar."[23] She was a member of many civic organizations, including the Social Security Advisory Committee, the State and National Defense Council, the American Association of Medical Social Workers, the National League of Nurses' Association, the Michigan Hospital Survey of Construction Program, the Michigan State Board of Registration for Nurses, the Michigan Hospital Association, and the Greater Detroit Hospital Association.[24]

Her first term as Mother Provincial of the Detroit Province extended to 1946. During these years her "constructive wizardry" was at its height, as she not only established a new province and college, but also helped others who wished to found their own institutions. In 1943 she assisted the Reverend Laval Landry, with the building of a new elementary school for Our Lady of LaSallette Parish in Berkley, Michigan.[25] In 1944 she supervised the construction of a five-story addition to Mt. Mercy Academy in Grand Rapids, Michigan.

During that period Mother Carmelita also conceived of and established Our Lady of Mercy, a girls' high school in the Detroit area. Between 1944 and 1945, she spent every spare moment studying the blueprints, revising the plans, and supervising the workers. She pressured and coaxed the crews into meeting the completion deadline, and on September 6, 1945, Our Lady of Mercy High School welcomed its first three hundred students.[26] Years later, a dramatic surge in enrollment necessitated that the high school relocate to a larger complex in Farmington Hills. Mercy College of Detroit acquired the old school, renamed it Marian Hall, and currently conducts many of its classes there.

Mother Carmelita served as Assistant Provincial Administrator of the Detroit Province from 1946 until 1952, continuing to pursue her dream of providing quality health care and education for everyone. She remained active in the establishment of new buildings, and in 1949, she supervised the opening of St. Ann Hospital in Algona, Iowa.[27] Although she routinely directed multi-million dollar projects, she never forgot to fight for the rights of individuals. Sister Mary Justin Sabourin, a colleague, describes how Mother Carmelita once pulled all the Mercy Hospitals in Michigan out of the Blue Cross system until the insurers agreed to pay the health care costs she demanded should be covered. They met her conditions within three days.[28] She also offered her organizational and nursing talents to a hospital in Sioux City, Iowa during a polio epidemic in the early 1950s. The hospital was swamped by a sudden influx of critically ill polio patients. Mother Carmelita assessed the situation and promptly opened an empty floor with the loyal assistance of her Iowa Sisters and a few nurses. On the first morning after her arrival on the scene, she had the hallways lined with iron lungs, the floor staffed with volunteers, and all the patients cared for.[29]

In 1952 Mother Carmelita was re-elected the Detroit Provincial Administrator and held that office until 1955. A four-million dollar expansion project for Detroit's St. Joseph Mercy Hospital in 1952 was the last of her building projects. Her community and colleagues showered honors upon her, including the 1953 Michigan Association Key for meritorious service throughout the state. In 1955 she was declared one of the Ten Most Distinguished Women in Detroit.[30] Her last years as provincial were spent with as much enthusiasm and civic achievements as her earlier years.

In 1955, at the age of 67, Mother Carmelita settled into semi-retirement. She insisted on remaining active, however, and spent much of her time serving in the Mercy hospitals of Dubuque and Sioux City, Iowa, and Ann Arbor, Michigan.[31] Her lighter work schedule enabled her to interact with her patients more personally. While still actively engaged in the work of supervising out-patient clinics, directing the purchasing departments, ministering to patients, and conducting religious services, she died at Mercywood Hospital in Ann Arbor on January 21, 1962.[32]

Her funeral was held at St. Scholastica Church in Detroit, located across the street from the college she had founded. Great and small gathered to pay their respects for the personal charity and community service of a lifetime. Many of her spontaneous acts of generosity were unknown to her colleagues until that time, because she considered sharing whatever she had to be natural, and therefore, nothing to waste time talking about.[33]

Remembering her, a contemporary member of her order notes that "charity was the very essence of her being", but there was much more to Mother Carmelita than the qualities ascribed to the traditional nun.[34] She possessed a powerful ability to feel the pulse of the community and to respond to that pulse on a grand scale. Her creative power sprang from an unorthodox integration of compassion, intuition, and nurturance with organization, management, and industry. Her legacy lives on in the hearts and minds of her sisters and of those who are educated in the schools she founded.

NOTES

[1]"Mother Manning Dies," Obituary The Detroit Free Press, 23 January 1962.

[2]"Life of Selfless Service," (Farmington Hill, Michigan: Religious Sisters of Mercy Archives), n. d. and n. p.

[3]Mary Lucille Middleton and Marjorie Allen, The Quality of Mercy, (Royal Oak, Michigan: Linden Press, 1980,) p. 191.

[4]"Mother Carmelita Manning," The Campus Reporter (Marygrove College of Detroit), 23 January 1962.

[5]Middleton and Allen, p. 179.

[6]Mary Justin Sabourin, R.S.M., Farmington Hills, Michigan, personal interview, 20 March 1987.

[7]Middleton and Allen, p. 192.

[8]Middleton and Allen, p. 183.

[9]"Mother Mary Carmelita Manning, R.S.M.," (Farmington Hills, Michigan: Religious Sisters of Mercy Archives), n. d. and n. p.

[10]Dr. Juliana Thomson, Detroit, Michigan, personal interview, 5 March 1987.

[11]Middleton and Allen, p. 198.

[12] "Mother Mary Carmelita Manning, R.S.M.,"

[13] The Campus Reporter

[14] "A Nurse Is Honored," (Farmington Hills, Michigan: Religious Sisters of Mercy Archives), n. d. and n. p.

[15] Obituary, The Detroit Free Press.

[16] Sabourin.

[17] Sabourin.

[18] Thomson.

[19] Middleton and Allen, p. 207.

[20] Thomson.

[21] Mary Carmelita Manning, R.S.M., "Incentive for a Career," (Farmington Hills, Michigan: Religious Sisters of Mercy Archives), p. 2.

[22] "Mother Carmelita, R.S.M., Given Distinguished Award" unidentified newspaper), 25 June 1942.

[23] Middleton and Allen, p. 192-193.

[24] "Mother Carmelita Manning, R.S.M.,".

[25] Middleton and Allen, p. 205.

[26] Middleton and Allen, p. 207.

[27] Middleton and Allen, p. 213.

[28] Sabourin.

[29] Mary Ruth Gorman, R.S.M., Farmington Hills, Michigan, personal interview, 20 March 1987.

[30] Middleton and Allen, p. 192.

[31] Obituary, The Detroit Free Press,.

[32] "Life of Selfless Service,".

[33] Thomson.

[34] Mary Herbert Cannon, R.S.M., Farmington Hills, Michigan, personal interview, 20 March 1987.

ANA CLEMENC (1888 – 1956)

ANA CLEMENC
HEROINE OF THE COPPER MINES

Virginia Law Burns

Ana Klobuchar Clemenc's life began as first-born child to Slovene immigrants in the thriving mining town of Redjacket, Michigan. The time was 1888, the same year Jane Addams was in Britain observing English methods of helping immigrants to become acclimated to their new environment. The most successful seemed to be "settlement houses," which Miss Addams used, with modification, when she returned to Chicago. Clemenc was later to hear the great lady speak when she toured the country urging social reform.

Ana Klobuchar grew up as a copper miner's daughter, possessing traditional native qualities of spirit and strong independence inherited from her European ancestors. Her mother added to the meager miner's wages by catering, midwifing, and laundering. The young girl did not attend high school, yet she was well educated. Her eighth grade diploma meant that she was better equipped than most laborer's children, who usually dropped out of school much earlier to supplant their family's income. Clemenc avidly followed Eugene Debs into Socialism and labor reform, along with other notables such as Mother Mary Harris Jones and Upton Sinclair.

By the time the miner's daughter was twenty-five years old, she was a miner's wife, Mrs. Joseph Clemenc. Ana had flashing brown eyes and long hair, dark as an unlighted mine shaft, and stood more than six feet tall! She and her husband lived from "peda to peda" (payday to payday) in the heavily populated Upper Peninsula area called Calumet. Mine wages were low, and conditions underground grew more and more dangerous. Mine captains cheated the workers, especially those who had not mastered the English language. The men had no one to whom they could air their grievances.

Discontent and unrest grew in the mine community until the summer of 1913. By this time, many workers had joined the Western Federation of Miners and were ready to strike. Clemenc was more than ready.

Through that summer and the bitter, snowy winter, she starred as a symbol of the miners' struggle to be free of the paternalistic mine owners, dishonest foremen, and pitiful wages. Her enthusiastic leadership of the miners' daily parades, in which she carried a flag as large as she was, encouraged the strikers. They knew it was important to be seen and heard, so they spent hours in the streets trying to persuade mine workers to honor the strike--to not go down the shafts or into the pumphouses.

One morning in late September, Charles Moyer, President of the Western Federation of Miners, stood near the Redjacket mine location on Seventh Street with Clemenc whose tall figure and strong voice were very much in the public's eyes and ears. Today, she and the union chief were with other strikers, gathered at the curbside.

"It's hard to keep my hand off the scabs," Clemenc said, more to herself than her companion. She drew the collar of her long, dark woolen coat closer around her throat. As the sun rose higher, more and more nonstriking workers, lunchbuckets in hand, appeared.

She called to a miner as he approached, "Where are you going, partner?"

The man slowed. "To work." Clemenc stifled a impulse to scold and, softening her attitude, said, "Not in the mine, are you?"

"You bet I am!"

Clemenc began her sales talk, by now well-polished, and the miner, flattered by her attention, chatted amiably. Presently the miner's wife stepped forward and touched his arm. He tipped his hat to the ardent strike leader and, eyes downcast, hurried toward the shaft entrance.

"Annie, with the C & H mine President Shaw refusing to leave his comforts in Boston and owner MacNaughton turning his back on arbitration," Moyer said, "Things are bound to get worse before they get better. We must be prepared for that."

"Yes, I know," Clemenc said, her forehead wrinkling. "I have no children, yet we're finding it harder each day to make the food stretch. If it wasn't for the few dollars I have coming in from my boarders, I don't know what we'd do. Even families who have gardens are running low because they share with the rest of us."

Moyer shuffled his feet and looked at the barren trees and gray skies.

"Don't you usually have snow by this time?"

"Sure do," Clemenc said, "We're lucky so far. At least the streets are clear for marching."

Presently two Slavs, one of whom she knew, approached. Running to face the pair she cried, "Oh George! You are not going to work, are you? Don't allow that bad woman (his wife) to drive you to work. Stick with us and we will stick with you!"

The man hesitated. His face flushed, and he ran a rough hand through his blond hair. Embarrassment changed to determination, and he left his friend to step out of the stream of workers. Clemenc didn't try to keep track of her unsuccessful attempts, but she felt a childlike delight when she was able to convince a man not to cross the picket line.

Strike breakers, never far from any public action by the union members, materialized. Two of them grabbed George by the shoulders and propelled him along the street.

"You coward," they accused, "Are you going back because a woman told you not to go to work?"

George, not so much angered at being called a coward as resentful at being pushed around, dropped his precious lunchpail and fought back. Immediately, six more deputies jumped into the fracas and George found himself being dragged toward the mine.

The swarm of men, which were beginning to look like ants taking a prize bit of food to a hole in the ground and paid no heed to the defiant Clemenc who shouted and gestured after them. Her church training notwithstanding, she was familiar with the coarse language of the laborers and knew how to use it. She was in good form that morning.

"Annie, you have to get away from here."

The man's voice sounded from behind her. It was clear, unemotional, commanding. Startled, she wheeled to face an army officer, a stranger.

"No, I'm not going. I have a right to stand here and quietly ask the scabs not to go to work."

The officer politely ignored the fact that she had been anything but quiet.

"You will have to get into the auto," the officer said. Clemenc drew herself up and with crossed arms assessed her position. Somewhere a dog barked, a mine whistle blew. She smelled the oily exhaust of the chugging automobile engine, saw the officer's aides sitting inside the carriage.

"I won't go until you tell me the reason," she said. Because she had lived these past weeks under the constant threat of arrest, she felt no alarm.

Without warning, two of the commander's aides appeared on either side of her and, half-pulling, half-carrying, hoisted her onto the seat of the first automobile she had ever been in.

Outraged, the tall woman pounded her feet on the car's floorboards. Powerless as her position was, she continued to stamp her feet and demand an explanation, but the aides only climbed into the vehicle and slammed the heavy, black, half-doors. At a signal from the ranking officer, the driver turned the wooden steering wheel toward the city jail.

Clemenc was soon to learn that her abductor was General Peter Abbey, commander of the state militia. He leaned back and looked squarely at his captive.

"Why don't you stay at home?"

Annie stopped banging her heels and returned his stare.

"I won't stay home," she said. "My work is here. Nobody can stop me. I'm going to keep at it until this strike is won for the workers."

The car came to a stop, and the aides escorted Clemenc into the "dirty little Calumet jail," words she used later to describe her experiences. She was charged with assault and battery.

"I haven't assaulted or battered anybody!" she protested to the jail clerk. "These men assaulted me! I was standing quietly, rallying the men to hang together. I wasn't breaking any law!"

The clerk looked over his glasses at the defiant organizer and the soldiers standing by.

"I wondered how long it would be before you'd land in here again," he said, not unkindly.

When the Christmas season arrived and the few hundred remaining strikers had nothing for their families, Ana Clemenc and other union women formed the Women's Alliance and found ways to provide extra food, small gifts, and needed clothing for the hard-pressed families. They planned a party for all union members, and from that gathering came the terrible Italian Hall Tragedy. Seventy-four persons, thirty-nine of them children, were crushed to death in a panic within the hall's stairwell after someone had erroneously cried, "Fire!" Testimony later revealed that several witnesses had seen a small chimney fire on the outside of the building, but there had never been any danger.

Soon after, Ella Reeve Bloor, a union socialist and journalist who was one of Clemenc's idols, took her as a companion speaker on a train tour of the Midwest, hoping to raise money for the union and strikers. They came home, however, with less money than they had started with.

Clemenc's return meant she had to pay fines and serve jail time for her previous convictions. During these times, her marriage had failed, and she had fallen in love with an editor of a Slovene newspaper.

In April 1914, she left Calumet and joined journalist Frank Shavs in Chicago, where they were married. Their only child, a daughter, was born that year.

The strike had won the miners only two concessions—an eight-hour day and better grievance procedures. Union victory was to come later. Yet "Tall Annie" was not dispirited or bitter. She remained active in socialist causes, but never again took to the streets to organize for labor.

Life thereafter was not kind to Clemenc. Her new husband became an alcoholic, mean and stingy; their daughter Darwina lost an arm in an auto accident. For years, the union's "Joan of Arc" worked at two jobs.

Ana Klobuchar Clemenc Shavs died in the same house in which she had lived for thirty-three years. Her death certificate reads: Occupation—hatmaker.

Ana Shavs was an instigator, flag bearer and inspirational leader for the nine months the desperate copper miners of

Ana Clemenc 203

Calumet refused to work. She was a glorious display of fireworks in the dark skies of the conflict. Her colors exploded briefly, yet remain brilliant in the memories of Michigan's Upper Peninsula.

NOTE: Juvenile biographer Virginia Burns has provided a bibliography instead of footnotes.

BIBLIOGRAPHY

American Great Crises in History, Vol IX and X. Americanization Dept. of Veterans of Foreign Wars of the U.S., Chicago, Ill. 1925.

Andrews, Clarence A. "'Big Annie' and the 1913 Michigan Strike," Michigan History, '57 (Spring 1973): 53-68.

Bloor, Ella Reeve, We Are Many, (New York: International Publishers, 1940). An autobiography of the prominent journalist.

History of the Diocese of Sault Saint Marie and Marquette Village and Calumet, Michigan. Souvenir Centennial Book, 1875-1975.

Klobuchar, Frank. Ana's only surviving close relative. Letters. Photographs, family documents and oral recollections.

Miners' Bulletin. Calumet, Mich. Oct. 2, 1913, p. 1.

Molek, Ivan (John), Slovene Immigrant History, 1900-1950. Translated by Bary Molek. (Delaware: Dover Press 1979).

Sullivan, William A. "The 1913 Revolt of the Michigan Copper Miners", Michigan History 43 (Sept. 1959): pp. 294-314.

Thurner, Arthur W. Calumet Copper and People: History of a Michigan Mining Community, 1864-1970, Hancock, Michigan, 1974.

Thurner, Arthur W., Rebels on the Range: The Michigan Copper Miners Strike of 1913-1914. Lake Linden, Michigan: Forster Press, 1984.

MARGUERITE LOFFT DE ANGELI (1889 – 1987)

MARGUERITE LOFFT DE ANGELI
WRITER AND ILLUSTRATOR FOR CHILDREN

K. Fawn Knight

"I must do something before I am thirty-five."

In 1981, while speaking to a group of eighth-grade students, Marguerite de Angeli described her life as a young matron and mother of three. "And I think I said to myself," she commented, "I must do something before I am thirty-five."[1] The "something" de Angeli began was a fifty-year career as an author and illustrator of children's books, for which she received numerous honors, including the prestigious Newbery Award and the Lewis Carroll Shelf Award.

Marguerite Lofft de Angeli was born in Lapeer, Michigan, on March 14, 1889. Her parents, George Lofft and Ruby Tuttle Lofft, had moved home to Lapeer, where both their families lived, shortly after their marriage. The second of three children, Marguerite was born in the Tuttle family home which still stands at 937 North Main Street. Grandfather Lofft's blacksmith shop was a well-known feature of Lapeer life at the turn of the century, and his craftsmanship may still be seen in the ironwork gates to Mt. Hope cemetery in that community.

De Angeli incorporated stories about her parents and grandparents into Copper-Toed Boots (1938), a novel for children set in turn-of-the-century Lapeer.[2] Aunts, uncles, and other relatives lived in the Lapeer community as well. De Angeli's childhood memories, recounted years later in her autobiography Butter at the Old Price (1971), were of a blissfully secure and happy family.

Music, art, and drawing seem to have been early impulses in her life. Her father, the town photographer, kept a studio in which he also displayed samples of his work in pastels, primarily chalk portraits. De Angeli later recalled that she remembered a longing to create books from as young as age three.[3]

The family's economic situation seems to have been uncertain during their years in Lapeer. They moved from house to house several times, and once moved briefly to Chicago. In 1902, when Marguerite was thirteen, her father's work with Eastman Kodak took the family to Philadelphia where she was to spend most of her adult life with only occasional sojourns in Michigan.

In 1910, Marguerite married John ("Dai") de Angeli, a musician and member of the Philadelphia Symphony Society, forerunner of the Philadelphia Orchestra. Prior to her marriage, she had seriously pursued an operatic career, auditioning successfully for Oscar Hammerstein and winning a place in a company scheduled to tour Great Britain. In keeping with the expectations of the time, however, and influenced by her parents' counsel, she gave up her musical career in favor of what they assured her would be the more meaningful and satisfying choice of rearing a family.[4]

The first years of the de Angeli marriage must have been difficult ones. Dai de Angeli took a position representing the Edison Company in Canada, a job involving frequent transfers and travel. By 1913, three of their six children had been born, and in 1914, with Canadian troops already mobilizing for the war in Europe, the de Angelis decided to return to the States. Shortly after settling in Collingswood, New Jersey, just outside Philadelphia, their infant daughter, Catherine, died suddenly. Within a year, Dai de Angeli had accepted a position in Detroit, moving the young family yet again.

Wartime shortages, the great influenza epidemic of 1918, and the death of de Angeli's sister Nina all contributed to the anxiety of these years. It was not until the early 1920's, when they were once again living in Collingswood, that the de Angelis achieved a measure of stability in their lives. They lived in Collingswood for several years before the hardships of the Depression forced yet another move. Although at times de Angeli's income from her writing and illustrating was the sole support for an extended family of nine, the family never faced quite the same disruption as in earlier years. They remained in Pennsylvania, and later she and her husband lived in Philadelphia proper.

None of de Angeli's recorded comments reveal any fundamental dissatisfaction with her choice of domestic life; however, some yearning for a broader sphere must have remained. She continued to sing publicly on occasion and once took a series of art lessons. In accepting the Newbery Award for 1950, she commented:

> "It wasn't until I was married and the mother of three children that the impelling drive to draw became so insistent that it couldn't be denied."[5]

In 1921, when she was 32, she met artist Maurice Bower and so began "the fulfillment of the dream of years."[6] Bower, an illustrator who had trained in the tradition of Howard Pyle and N.C. Wyeth, became a valued mentor for de Angeli. He encouraged her to submit a portfolio to a publisher of religious materials, and thus her first commissioned work as an illustrator was for a children's Sunday School magazine. Over the next fifteen years, she worked steadily as an illustrator and later as a writer for several publishers and religious houses as well as for the major women's periodicals of the day, for children's magazines such as St. Nicholas Magazine and The American Girl, and for a number of prominent writers for children. A researcher trying to establish a definitive bibliography of de Angeli's work has identified more than sixty stories and over thirty books illustrated by her over the years in addition to those she wrote herself.[7]

In 1935, a publisher commissioned her to write a book for young readers. Ted and Nina Go to the Grocery Store (1935) was the result, followed the next year by Ted and Nina Have a Happy Rainy Day. With these publications, de Angeli's career took a major turn. For the next four decades, she wrote and illustrated some twenty-five books of her own for children.

Dai de Angeli died in 1969, just a few months before their sixtieth wedding anniversary. His wife continued throughout the next decade to keep up a series of public appearances and to write and publish. In 1981, her last book appeared, a collection titled Friendship and Other Poems. The same year, she served as Grand Marshal in Lapeer's sesquicentennial celebration. In 1986, when ill health forced Marguerite de Angeli to break up housekeeping, she and her family donated her archives to the Lapeer Public Library which was renamed the Marguerite de Angeli Public Library in her honor.

De Angeli received some of the most prestigious book awards in the United States: Caldecott Honor Book Awards in 1945 and 1955 for Yonie Wondernose and the Book of Nursery and Mother Goose Rhymes respectively and the Newbery Medal in 1950 for The Door in the Wall; and Mewbery Honor Book Award in 1957 for The Black Fox of Lorne. She is one of only a handful of artists ever to be awarded these two prestigious honors as both an illustrator (Caldecott) and as a

Marguerite Lofft de Angeli

writer (Newbery). In 1961 she received the Lewis Carroll Shelf Award, and numerous other awards came to her as a writer over the years. Both Michigan and Pennsylvania have honored her as their own. Her ninetieth birthday, for example, was declared by Governor William Milliken of Michigan to be "Marguerite de Angeli Day." In 1985, she was inducted into the Michigan Women's Hall of Fame.

Perhaps de Angeli's most significant contribution to children's literature was a series of books which sympathetically portray the lives of racial and religious minorities. The first of these, Henner's Lydia (1936), tells of a contemporary Amish child, the first American storybook for young elementary children ever to portray this group. Petite Suzanne (1937), Skippack School (1939), and Up the Hill (1942) deal respectively with contemporary French-Canadian, Mennonite, and Polish youngsters. For young readers, she also wrote novels of historical fiction which deal with minority groups: Thee Hannah (1940) portrays a Quaker girl whose family assists in the Underground Railroad and Elin's Amerika (1942) tells of a Swedish girl whose family immigrates to New Amsterdam (New York) in the 1600's.

Each of these books was meticulously researched, with particular care taken to recreate the distinctive vocabulary and cadences of each group's dialect. The books have in common a sense of happy childhood and an emphasis on the small problems of daily life which all children must overcome, regardless of their cultural backgrounds. Often the protagonists must resolve difficulties engendered by their own failure to act responsibly. In her public comments, de Angeli emphasized early experiences which taught her how much all people have in common, regardless of ethnic background.

> We discovered, as others have, how little basic difference there is; that it is only in the non-essentials

that we differ; what we have for breakfast, and how we greet our parents, or a different way of expressing the same homely truths, those bits of wisdom that have grown out of ages of experience.[8]

The emphasis on universal experience, however, did not obscure the distinctive beliefs and practices of each cultural group. The enormous popularity of these works can be seen in the fact that a whole series of dolls were modeled after various heroines from her books.[9]

In the whirligig of time, the very qualities which were most distinguished in de Angeli's early works have brought her criticism in recent years. Bright April (1946), in particular, has been controversial. April is a young black girl whose life revolves around her family and her Brownie troop. To some modern readers, April's life has seemed to be a bland, idealized portrait of a middle-class family with little relationship to the realities of black life and culture. Particularly disturbing from this perspective is the counsel adults give April when she encounters racial prejudice: essentially, April must be as clean, as neat, as polite, as good as she can in order to prove her white peers that she is worthy of acceptance. Similar concerns might be raised about the portrayal of Native Americans in Elin's Amerika and the traditional, domestic orientation toward women's roles in her books. Although most of de Angeli's books have remained in print, it is possible that these values may come to so date them that they will no longer be widely read; however, current unfavorable criticism should not obscure their very genuine contribution.

Bright Angel was published in 1946, in the wake of World War II. The racial integration of military units, instituted by President Roosevelt, had been a matter of public debate only a few years earlier. De Angeli's original intention was to write

Marguerite Lofft de Angeli

a book about a biracial child, a concept so radical that her editor refused to consider it. Even the scene in which a white child climbs into bed with April seemed far more daring when written than it would today. Bright April is a landmark book, the first mainstream book for young children to unequivocally portray white racial prejudice, the first to center entirely on a black family, the first to use a three-dimensional black character as the protagonist, the first to explicitly condemn the barriers which kept black young people from achieving economic equality.

It was historical fiction for older children, however, which brought de Angeli the greatest recognition as a writer, especially The Door in the Wall (1949) and Black Fox of Lorne (1956). The Door in the Wall, for which de Angeli received the 1950 Newbery Award, is set in 13th century England and tells the story of a young boy, left crippled and alone in plague-stricken London, and his adventures before he is reunited with his parents. De Angeli often states her themes explicitly. In The Door in the Wall, Brother Luke tries to encourage young Robin with an analogy to a castle wall. The wall becomes a metaphor for obstacles encountered in life:

> "Dost remember the long wall that is about the garden of thy father's house?" inquires the Friar. "Dost remember, too, the wall about the Tower or any other wall? ...Have they not all a door somewhere? ...Remember, ...[t]hou has only to follow the wall far enough and there will be a door somewhere."[10]

This recurring concern for values reflects de Angeli's belief that the writer of children's literature has a responsibility to her audience. She once wrote an admirer of hers:

Every book I have done was considered from every standpoint, and I puzzled over words, trying to be sure they conveyed my meaning and would have no adverse influence on a child. So I am very happy that they are useful.[11]

That books should be useful to the child, morally and spiritually encouraging, was a fundamental goal of her work. Although she viewed the "sickening, sentimental" treatment of Jesus by a certain religious group with disdain, she consistently placed her work within a Christian framework.[12] In later years, she selected and illustrated The Old Testament (1960) and the Book of Favorite Hymns (1963).

It was, in fact, as an illustrator that de Angeli first worked, and drawing and painting remained a central focus in her creative life. Pencil and colored pencil were favorite media, but she also worked both in water color and in crayon. Readers who are new to her work will almost certainly note her portrayal of children in their daily activities. There is a sameness to the children, certainly, with their characteristic heart-shaped faces, but also a distinctive gaiety and delicacy. Her own children, when they were young, were frequent models. In fact, she once commented:

> When I had the children, I found out how to draw children and I studied anatomy when I bathed them. Even their bones and how they connected and so forth....[13]

Later on, her granddaughter, Kate de Angeli Creitz, became the model for the toddler in de Angeli's classic Book of Nursery and Mother Goose Rhymes (1954). Yet it is not the individuality of any one child which is conveyed in her works as much as the universal child--inquiring, vulnerable, and eager. Equally important in the illustrations is her meticulous recreation of setting. Whether of 13th century London or 20th century Philadelphia, her illustrations show a fine attention to detail which establishes locale and mood. The illustrations for The Door in the Wall, for example, show not only Robin's and Brother Luke's costumes, but the gargoyles carved into the stone above their heads and even the heavy nails studding the door behind them. Her sketches and water color studies preserved in the Lapeer library show an interest in flowers and plants which is reflected in Nursery and Mother Goose Rhymes and A Pocketful of Posies (1961), as well as incidentally in the details of her other works.

Those who knew Marguerite de Angeli personally when she was older found her so approachable and modest that she earned the nickname "Everybody's Grandmother."[14] With over twenty full-length books of her own and a prolific career as an illustrator, she left an impressive legacy for a young mother who worried, at 35, that she must hurry and make a start on a career.

NOTES

[1] de Angeli, Marguerite Lofft. "Acceptance Speech for the Newbery Award," Horn Book Magazine, June-July, 1950, p. 344.

[2] de Angeli, Marguerite Lofft. Copper-Toed Boots. New York: Doubleday, 1938. Additional books by de Angeli will be cited parenthetically in the text. Publisher is Doubleday unless otherwise noted.

[3] Anderson, William T. "A Visit to the Classroom of William Anderson at White Junior High School." 25 May 1970. Typescript. Marguerite de Angeli Public Library, Lapeer, Michigan; p. 30. William Anderson was a teacher in Lapeer at the time of this visit. He has since published a biography of de Angeli and numerous articles about her.

[4] de Angeli, Marguerite Lofft. Butter at the Old Price. New York: Doubleday, 1971, pp. 52-53.

[5] de Angeli, Marguerite Lofft. "Acceptance Speech," p. 344.

[6] de Angeli, Marguerite Lofft. Butter at the Old Price. New York: Doubleday, 1971, p. 88.

[7] Miles, William. Letter to Laura C. Strauss. 5 May 1986. Marguerite de Angeli Public Library, Lapeer, Michigan. Miles is the coordinator of Reader Services for the Clarke Historical Library in Mt. Pleasant, Michigan. De Angeli was extremely prolific, and these numbers continue to rise as new (unsigned) illustrations are identified.

[8] de Angeli, Marguerite Lofft. "Acceptance Speech," p. 346.

[9] The Hedwick dolls, which were copyrighted, included Henner's Lydia, Elin of Elin's Amerika, April of Bright April, and others. Some were cloth, some bisque. Collectors' items today, examples can be seen in the Marguerite de Angeli collection in Lapeer, Michigan.

[10] de Angeli, Marguerite Lofft. The Door in the Wall. New York: Doubleday, 1959. p 16.

[11] de Angeli, Marguerite Lofft. Letter to William T. Anderson. n.d. Marguerite de Angeli Public Library, Lapeer, Michigan.

[12] Butter at the Old Price. p. 33.

[13] Anderson, William T. p. 38.

[14] Anderson, William T. "Marguerite de Angeli: 'Everybody's Grandmother' Has a Birthday." Jack and Jill, March 1982. pp. 12-14.

LOLETA DAWSON FYAN (1894 -)

LOLETA DAWSON FYAN
STATE LIBRARIAN

Emma Shore Thornton

From 1941-1961 Loleta Dawson Fyan was in the forefront of an important pioneering movement. As head of the Michigan State Library and secretary to the State Board of Libraries, she advanced the cause of libraries and the cause of general education as well. Under her leadership, library services were made available to literally millions of people who had previously had no such services. Moreover, the quality of service was improved by better training of librarians and by better access to materials. Fyan's library career--marked by her distinctive personality, strong character, and charisma--became synonymous with library extension.

Loleta Irene Dawson was born May 14, 1894 in a small hamlet on the outskirts of Clinton, Iowa, to Albert and Phoebe DeGroat Dawson. Her family background had an important influence on her life and career. From her forebears came the influence of a pioneering spirit. Her maternal grandparents, Minerva and Zachariah DeGroat, migrated from western New York State as newly-weds, traveling via the Erie Canal and overland to Iowa in 1858. They acquired a sizeable farm, made a good life for themselves and their family and, possessed of an extraordinary sense of responsibility and civic interest, contributed greatly to the making of the community of Preston, Iowa. Fyan's father, Albert Dawson, grew up in straightened circumstances. He was raised by his grandparents and his grandfather was a disabled Civil War veteran. Out of near-poverty, Dawson rose to be acclaimed as "a self-made man." But he was more than that term may imply. Like the DeGroats, Dawson had concerns for other people and saw advantages in cooperative endeavors that contributed to the common good. From the Dawson-DeGroat heritage two sets of traits or values emerge; individually, Loleta Fyan's ancestors were proud, aggressive, and enterprising; socially, they were civic-minded, benevolent, and humanistic. This heritage was transmitted to Loleta.

Fyan was most obviously influenced by her father. He propelled himself from small beginnings to become secretary to Iowa's senior U.S. senator and then, on his own merits, was elected to congress. His energy furnished Loleta with an out-of-the-ordinary childhood. The atmosphere of politics came with the air she breathed, and that atmosphere was as much "home" to her as were any of the revolving places of residency the family occupied during her growing years. When Fyan was later asked about her beginnings, she invariably made one and only one reply: "My father was a congressman and I went to school in Washington, D.C."[1] In that statement she summed up her own identification with pride and power as well as the indelible imprint which her father's prowess and the nation's capital made on her. The imprint was often evident in the course of her life, when she would say, "Politics is my life."[2]

Loleta Dawson Fyan provided her own record of her life as a schoolgirl and as a maturing individual in fifteen volumes of diaries that cover the years from 1911 to 1925. From her own accounts, it is possible to understand how the influences of her past shaped her view of herself and, to some extent, defined the course of her future. After graduation from high school, her parents sent her to Wellesley College. The word "sent" fits the situation, for almost everything about these four years at Wellesley confirms the conclusion that she did not really know why she was there, though a bit of magic known as a diploma dangled at the end. Wellesley, then forty years old, had a notable reputation for the quality and range of its professional faculty, almost all of whom were women with advanced degrees. Loleta Dawson Fyan remained virtually untouched by them. Academically, she was a mediocre student throughout. She got a taste of "dull" subject matter, a taste of affluent Boston, a small taste of feminism, and a larger penchant for girlish crushes. While she continued to honor and respect her elders, she followed her natural inclination in seeking friendly relations with her dormitory peers. It was in the course of following that natural bent that Fyan's real college education took hold and led her out of self-absorption into a growing understanding of interpersonal relations, group processes, and organization. This learning was a course of action but not a course in the college curriculum.

Few would call it a course—unusual, unaccredited, and thoroughly dynamic as it was. It had no program of study, no measurement of progress, no instructor. It proceeded loosely on a trial and error basis. Only later analysis of Fyan's behavior, as described in her diary, discloses the outlines of that course. It began during her first week as a Freshman, when, to her consternation, she was appointed as proctor of her floor in the dorm. She tried to resist the appointment. Like the other girls, she wanted to make friends with her peers, but how could she, when as proctor she had to keep her floor-mates in line and report their misdemeanors? Proctors normally were seen as enemies, not as friends. That became apparent at once, and Fyan found it disturbing. In time, however, in spite of the fact that girls at Wellesley saw her as "aloof," "cold," and sometimes "priggish," Fyan gained respect. She was fair-minded, and soon she had not only the respect but the friendship and even the admiration of her peers. Accordingly, she found herself in line for sundry positions in the dormitory organizational ladder. During her Senior year, she was president of Pomeroy Hall and also president of the Council of Residence Hall Presidents, an office of prestige. It is clear that in that position she assumed considerable responsibility, polished her organizational and interpersonal skills, and helped to advance the cause of student self-government, a fledgling idea in that era. Because of what Fyan made of this opportunity for leadership and because she absorbed so much from it that affected her eventual education, this course of action was more valuable than any college course.

After college came more than a year of disaster in a teaching situation for which she was ill-suited. Then she reluctantly became an apprentice, mending books at the Davenport Public Library. She fell into the hands of an outstanding library director who guided her on another upward path, which soon took her to Western Reserve University in Cleveland to study library science. There, Alice Tyler, the dean, saw the young woman as prime material. Dean Tyler nurtured her and Fyan graduated at the top of her class. Upon graduation, Tyler charged her with two commissions: to remain unmarried because marriage would destroy her career, and to become head of the State Library of Michigan within a very few years. She did not precisely follow the first charge, for she married Ted Fyan, but her marriage proved to be no hindrance to her career. In fact she gained a certain status that seemed to be important to her; and she gained a companion, an abettor, and a "househusband."

Upon graduation from Western Reserve in 1920, Loleta Fyan was hired by the Detroit Public Library and shortly was put in charge of the developmental program that led to the establishment of the Wayne County Library. She was a pioneer, the first librarian in one of the first county libraries in Michigan, which was likewise part of the early extension movement in the United States. What she did in the formation and development of the Wayne County Library system was first and foremost a pioneering feat for libraries in that locality; it was also a personal adventure and an investment in her future. From small, almost primitive beginnings, a federated system grew, and with it Fyan's career.

She began her career at an auspicious time for, in the 1920's, Americans were in an ebullient mood. The progressive movement in education, with its implications for democracy, gave impetus to library development. The rapid growth of industrialization in the Detroit area caused Wayne County's population to explode, and with that explosion came all the problems and needs of an unsettled people. In its sponsorship of the Wayne County library, the Detroit Public Library affirmed its progressive belief in libraries as effective agencies in solving problems and meeting needs and backed up its affirmation by providing seed money and the Scripps mansion for headquarters.[3] It became Fyan's job to prove the efficacy of the project.

As she began her new job, she correctly perceived the most significant aspects. She wrote in her diary:

> June 2, 1921: My first day--a ten-hour day on the road leads me to believe that my new job is going to be strenuous, full of problems and probabilities for a growth that will be hard to keep up with. It looks as if I would be traveling day and night, attending picnics, Mothers' Club meetings, giving talks at farmer's clubs-- gaining some of the earmarks of a politician and a

missionary, a strange combination...interurbaned to Redford the first thing this morning to see our latest center. It's in a little dressmaking shop that has only been open a month. Mrs. McCulley is in charge and has constructive ideas about her labor of love and is very interested. Two people have offered to help her, and she is going to speak to the Mothers' Club, which we heard on every side is the most up and coming organization in the town...She thinks they will be eager to back the proposition and provide a good case. She also suggested we get the board of commerce interested.

Coming from Redford we just caught a car to Dearborn, where we had a good dinner and met Miss Rogers, a county demonstrator. She chauffeured us about all afternoon--thru numerous towns making a stop in the lee of French Landing, where the city garbage is burned, and riding thru the sand to Mr. C.J. Schweitzer's farm. The Schweitzers are very nice farmer folk, Mr. and Mrs. and son Hubert, who is the librarian for the Sumpter Farm Club. We talked library and admired Mrs. Schweitzer's Sears-Roebuck wallpaper and her job of papering, enjoyed her cake and a donation of roses. We have a scheme to give book talks at the meetings of the farm club and take some books to the 4th of July picnic.

We came back to Dearborn via Belleville where the library is placed in a furniture store, but old Mr. Moon thinks it's more bother than it's worth to wait on people who want books.

She saw clearly that it was a strenuous job, full of problems and possibilities where all her skills as politician and missionary would be tested over and over again.

That first day was to become twenty years of days forming branches of the Wayne County Library system. The possibilities for growth were as wide as the county and as possible as local commitment and funding would support. It was her mission to begin where she found an opening, however primitive; to cultivate the appetite for a library; to form a constituency within the locality; to lead that constituency to be a political force; and to move the temporary status of a library into a permanent form. It was her job as politician to craft the program solidly, to persuade supporters and governmental officials wisely, and to guide the political process that would bring each library into reality. The formula worked. The county that had only three weak "canteens" and three private subscription libraries in 1920 had a central headquarters and 34 fully functioning branches in 1940.[4] Commercial library caretakers such as the Mr. Moon mentioned in her diary, who did not like to be bothered with the books, had long since been replaced by librarians. Though few of these were professionally trained, all had learned on the job and most of them had been personally tutored by Fyan or by members of her staff. Training of workers was a continuing necessity. By 1940 there were 145 staff members—145 times more than in 1921—and there were even a few professional librarians, specialists who headed reference or children's department. The county library budget was nearly 15 times larger than the first budget. In twenty years, thirty-four thriving libraries had grown from the smallest of beginnings. The local libraries were organized into a federated system wherein each unit maintained a program adapted to its own needs while it benefited from the economy, efficiency, and diversity offered by a central administration.

The twenty-year experience of building the county library system had been a ground for both training and testing. Her willingness to start small, balanced by her inbred need to "think big," proved to be an important key to progress. Her flair for strategy, for organization, and for public relations, all talents incipient at Wellesley, grew to be reliable ways of work. Her remarkable sense of how to present herself had become second nature. Throughout her career, colleagues remarked on this sense of presence; one saw her as "the unimpeachable duchess."[5] Her persona came to be a controlling force in her professional career and, combined with her other skills, proved equal to almost every challenge. The Wayne County Library had been established largely through her efforts and, because the county library extension movement was one of the rising movements of that day, she had also become nationally known by professional librarians in the American Library Association.

In 1934 she was made president of the Michigan Library Association (MLA) and, subsequently, Legislative Action chairman. In the course of these two assignments, she helped to draft and secure favorable legislative action on two key bills of great importance to the Library of Michigan and, likewise, to all existing and potential libraries of the state. Though members of the Michigan Library Association had long been concerned about the status of the State Library and, by implication, its effects on local libraries, never before had the group taken such a strong stand on legislation. Fyan was one of the chief activists for change and the legislative acts mandated the form that change would take.

The first law was a bold departure for the formerly meek, unaggressive librarians.[6] It required annual State Aid Grants to be administered by the State Library for the purposes of developing libraries in communities where there were none and of improving services in communities where libraries already had been established. The State Aid Grants could be made only after localities requesting service had met minimum requirements, designed to fit various levels of population, tax support, and other criteria. An equalizing factor in the law aided areas with weak tax bases. Thus, like grant proposals and demonstration projects instigated by other governmental groups, this legislation used the carrot (money promised) and stick (requirements to be met) approach. The boldness of this change was shown not only in the entry of libraries into active lobbying but also, and more significantly, in the future administrative potential of the legislation. For, following from that law, the State Library would almost certainly become a state-wide system. Heretofore, the Library of Michigan's chief responsibility had been to the legislature and governmental agencies. Though some services had gradually been extended to other segments—via the traveling library, special requests, and other services—the general public had previously had very limited access to the State Library's resources. Based on the new law, all this would change. The State Library would eventually become the nerve center for all public libraries in Michigan.

The second law was a partner of the first.[7] It provided for a State Board of Libraries whose task it was to set policies for the State Library and the state library system and, further, to oversee the administration of those policies. The Board was required to appoint a professionally trained and administratively experienced librarian to the post of State Librarian.

Both laws were departures from previous practice.[8] Never before had grants been made for the development of local libraries under the state budget. Never before had the State Librarian been possessed of both full professional qualifications and experience in administration. And never before had the State Librarian been appointed by procedures untainted by political partisanship. The MLA and librarians across the state had been pressing for these goals for more than twenty years. True, they honored the records of service of Harriet C. Tenney, Mary E. Spencer, and Mary Frankhauser (each appointed under political auspices) because each had discharged her responsibilities well, but now it was time for a professional library administrator. And it was many, many years past time for the Library to be removed from partisan politics.[9] Both achievements were hailed as great advances not only throughout Michigan but also throughout the United States, and the laws became models of library organization for other states. Given all the factors in the state library equation, including her not insignificant role in gaining the passage of those laws, the appointment of Loleta D. Fyan as State Librarian must have been a foregone conclusion. She took office on July 1, 1941.

The Library of Michigan was then located in the Lewis Cass building and was staffed by 33 employees. Fyan worked with this staff to reach her overriding goal of making the library service accessible to all Michigan residents. Studies showed that, in 1941, 20% of the people in the state had no access to library service.[10] Most of these lived in rural areas. In some cases, there was no library in an entire county and only very weak service for a whole region of counties. Fyan's challenge was to make library services available to all 83 counties, many of them far larger in area than Wayne County. She remained undaunted by the task set before her.

The staff grew. A consultant division was formed with responsibility for the extension and developmental program. These consultants functioned in much the same was as Fyan had functioned in Wayne County. The state library program moved forward step by step as struggling local groups became stronger, and joined into county library systems, and, subsequently, into regional systems. The goals of greater access and improved quality necessitated more and better training of library workers. Summer workshops were one form of intensive training employed, and hundreds of local librarians attended these workshops over the years, credits earned being necessary under the standards set by the State Aid Law. Fyan recalls how astonished she was upon meeting two librarians who had never been beyond the edge of the towns in which they lived.[11] Summer workshops were "open sesame" opportunities for such workers, just as library services could be for all.

Then, in February 1951, calamity struck. Arson caused "one of the greatest library fires in American history."[12] A tragic fire in the Lewis Cass building "dispossessed 14 state departments, partially paralyzed state government and changed the lives of thousands of people."[13] Poisonous fumes and sub-zero weather hampered the fire-fighters. The fire blazed out of control for three days, fueled by films, blue-print chemicals, and bales of paper. Six thousand gallons of water per second were poured into the building for 45 hours, soaking walls, loosening plaster, and cascading down through air vents and electrical conduits on book stacks in the five floors below the flames. Valuable books stood in two feet of water in the basement. Outside, sub-zero temperatures froze the cascading water as it fell, and the stone walls became encased in thick ice, making a ghostly scene.

Because of the enormity of the fire, the entire 375,000 book collection was subjected to very high humidity for almost a week, though efforts were made to protect it. For three days, only firemen were allowed inside. Then Fyan, "wearing a steel helmet, was the first woman to enter."[14] She immediately realized that a massive salvage operation would be necessary. Experts were called in and they said, "De-humidify immediately or lose everything!"[15] A field house owned by a state institution became a salvage center with its overhead heating ducts and fans and bleacher seats put to good use as 50,000 books were hauled there to dry. The staff, working in shifts around the clock, unpacked, set up, and frequently turned the books and leaves to speed the drying process. Pamphlets were hung on lines like so much washing.

In the meantime, back at the Cass building, tier after tier of water-soaked books had swelled so much they could not be removed from the shelves without the help of damaging tools. Here, another mass effort at dehumidifying began. Compressors ran for four weeks in this exhaustive operation. During the first week, 600 gallons of water per hour were squeezed out of the air in the Library section of the building. Library staff worked round the clock there, too.

Overall, it was a tremendous undertaking but the staff met the challenge selflessly and emerged from the experience with greater group cohesion. Of Fyan one staff member commented, "She was everywhere at once; she worked twenty hours of twenty-four for at least two weeks." Because of the joint efforts, relatively little was lost. "It was a miracle," Fyan said. It was a miraculous performance, but not the only miracle. Only six months prior to the fire, Fyan had, after long insistence, persuaded the state to increase the Library's insurance coverage.[16] When the emergency was over, she and others immediately began to dream of a new structure to house the Library of Michigan. This was in 1951. 1988 will bring that dream to reality.

The same year as the fire, Fyan became president of the 20,000 member American Library Association. In that role she was one of the chief advocates of the Federal Library Services Act, passed in 1956.[17] The law took its form from models such as the Michigan State Aid Law. Fyan's advocacy and effective lobbying were credited as significant. Thus, once again, her aims, her political skills, and her accomplishments had moved library extension forward. The Federal Library Services Act was a pace-setter and the foundation of the present federal law.

In 1961, Loleta Dawson Fyan's career came to a close. Her aims had always been high and open-ended. In twenty years' time, the accomplishments could not fully match those aims and make quality service available to everyone. The laws had emphasized rural development, and critics charged that the funds were inequitably distributed in favor of rural areas. The urban population had grown so rapidly that a million people still lacked service. Yet under Fyan's direction, the Library of Michigan had progressed in many ways. The Upper Peninsula Branch had been established, giving that area a state library base of its own. More public libraries had been established, and weak units strengthened and consolidated into county and regional systems. More professional librarians were employed and all library workers were more competent and better trained. Book collections had increased and so, too, had circulation. Perhaps only by contemplating what life would be like today if library service were as limited now as it was when Fyan became a librarian can an appreciation be gained of the progress. By the time she retired, the Library of Michigan had set the course for achieving that state-wide network of services she and others had envisioned. Today, sixteen area cooperatives make up that network. At all levels of service, the State Aid Law and the Federal Library Services and Construction Act had been the keys; leadership had turned the keys in the right locks.

From her own first days in Michigan, Fyan had given special meaning to the role of librarian as missionary and politician, in the best sense of those terms. She had sought the general well-being of all people in her efforts to lead them to use, appreciate, and enjoy libraries. She had used democratic political processes with non-partisan impartiality in her efforts to increase public awareness, to secure legislation, and to administer the library program. All of this was missionary. All, likewise, was political. As a policy-maker, she proved that well-crafted laws provided reliable charters for progress in library development. As an administrator, she showed that leadership and staff development were the keys to a successful library system. The thrust of the program initiated under her leadership continues today.

NOTES

[1] Loleta Fyan, personal interview, December 24, 1955. See Emma S. Thornton, Loleta and the Evergreen Tree, unpublished manuscript, p. 63.

[2] Fyan Personal interview, 1983; Thornton, p. 502.

[3] Frank B. Woodford, Parnassus on Main Street: a History of the Detroit Public Library. (Detroit: Wayne University Press, 1965), p. 371.

[4] Adam Strohm, "Wayne County Library: The First Twenty Years, 1920-1940," (Detroit: Wayne County Library Board, 1942), p. 12.

[5] Ruth Warncke, personal correspondence, March 1983, Thonton, p. 630.

[6] Michigan Public Acts, No. 315 (1937), p. 397.102f.

[7] Michigan Public Acts, No. 106 (1937), p. 397.1 f.

[8] John C. Larsen, A Study in Service: The Historical Development of the Michigan State Library and its Territorial Predecessor, the Legislative Council Library 1828-1941. (Ann Arbor: University Microfilms, Inc., 1967), p. 339.

[9] Larsen, p. 351.

[10] Charles R. Hoffer, "Public Library Service for Michigan Residents," Michigan Agricultural Experiment Station Quarterly Bulletin, Vol. 28, No. 1. (East Lansing, Michigan State College, 1943), pp. 1-9.

[11] Fyan, personal interview, October 1986, Thornton, p. 603.

[12]Don Hoenshell, "Firemen With Eerie Masks Battle Blaze," Lansing State Journal, 9 Feb, 1951.

[13]Loleta Fyan, "Michigan State Library: An Account of Water Damage and Salvage Operations," ALA Bulletin, Vol. 45, No. 1, p. 164.

[14]Thornton, p. 584.

[15]"Round-the-Clock Project Saving Library Collection," Lansing State Journal, 2 Feb, 1951.

[16]"Library Insurance Inadequate," Lansing State Journal, 8 June, 1950.

[17]Public Law 597 (84th Congress, 1956).

GENEVIEVE GILLETTE (1898 – 1986)

GENEVIEVE GILLETTE
LANDSCAPE ARCHITECT

Miriam Easton Rutz

E. Genevieve Gillette was a landscape architect who dedicated more than 60 years of her life to the preservation of Michigan's natural beauty for future generations. Professionally trained as a landscape architect, she was committed to stewardship of the natural landscape and to using scientific knowledge to create attractice public and private places for the enjoyment of all.[1] In the 1960s, she was one of very few women working in this field, so it was a measure of her significance that she was made a Fellow of the American Society of Landscape Architects in 1969.[2] Four others who were elected at the same time were men with international reputations in design and education. Her contributions were equally important. She was instrumental in the preservation of wilderness, the establishment of Michigan's state parks, the creation of national parks in the state, and the passage of bills and bonds for parks and recreation in both the state and the nation. Her commitment to the concept of stewardship of the land was complete. As the Natural Resource Commission said in a 1976 tribute, "She was the most effective lobbyist the state of Michigan has ever seen, and her remarkable energy and personality made her unforgettable to those who came into contact with her."[3]

234   *Historic Women of Michigan*

Gillette was born May 19, 1898, in Lansing, Michigan, and before her death in May of 1986, she had been named to the Michigan Conservation Hall of Fame and the Michigan Women's Hall of Fame and had had an interpretation and environmental center named in her honor. She was named to President Johnson's Citizens' Committee on Recreation and Natural Beauty, was chair of the National Conference on Scenic Roads, received an American Motors Conservation Award and Holiday Magazine's Award for Beautiful America, was made a distinguished alumni of Michigan State University, received an honorary doctoral degree from Albion College, and earned the respect of three governors and the legislature of the state of Michigan.[4]

How did she do it? "I didn't do it alone!" was always her answer. Others said it was the way she banged her cane on the ground and shouted, "Now listen here young man...." Still others said it was the way she laughed, the stories she told, the friends she kept, the letters she wrote, the phone calls she made, the courage she had. All would agree it was hard work, dedication, years of commitment to one idea, and total selflessness. She was a practical, Midwest farm girl whose father had instilled in her a love of nature. He died when she was 16, and her mother became a financial planner to put her only child through college. Gillette never married but cared for her mother and nurtured many young professionals. Her story shows it is possible to achieve one's goals through working for political change.

Gillette's professional career began after she graduated from Michigan Agricultural College in 1920 with a major in horticulture and landscape architecture. She went to work for Jens Jensen, a well-known landscape architect in Chicago, remembered as the father of the Chicago Park System.[5] At this time, he was president of the Friends of the Native Landscape, a conservation organization in Illinois which was involved with preliminary planning for a state park system. The first thing Gillette saw when she arrived at his office was a big sheet of paper covered with crayon scrawls. As she was staring at it, Mr. Jensen walked in and said, "You wouldn't be able to tell what that is?" She replied, "No, I guess I wouldn't." He told her it was the beginning concept for a state park at Starred Rock. As his assistant, she soon learned everything about his conservation efforts. She was in awe of this great man and in sympathy with his philosophy of design. Mr. Jensen kept asking her, "Why don't you get up a state park system in Michigan? You've got lots of resources over there and you ought to have a state park system."[6] With his encouragement, whenever she visited her mother in Lansing, she also visited P.J. Hoffmaster, who became Director of the Department of Conservation (now known as the Department of Natural Resources). He had been a student with her at Michigan State University and was working for the state to develop a state park system. At the time, Michigan had one state park, a small area that is now incorporated into Sleeping Bear Dunes National Lakeshore. The two of them talked enthusiastically together about a park system and how to acquire land.

After two years, she left Jensen's office to return to Michigan. She began to work for Breitmeyer Flower Company, a Detroit florist and nursery business. She maintained her friendship with Jensen, however, and he asked her to organize a Michigan meeting for the Friends of the Native Landscape. As a result of that meeting, an area of about 350 acres near Ludington was given to the state for a park. At the time, Gillette and Hoffmaster wondered, "What on earth will anybody do with 350 acres?"[7] She was thrilled, however, because it was now public land and she had been instrumental in obtaining it. Her efforts in conservation were beginning.

Gillette's friendship with Hoffmaster was of great value to the state of Michigan because they were both interested in acquiring land for state parks. Peter J. Hoffmaster became known throughout the nation as a leader in conservation and recreation. He was Director of Conservation for Michigan from 1934 until his death in 1951. He launched Michigan's State Park System in 1922 and was a strong advocate of reforestation, acquiring large state holdings in southeastern Michigan as well as in the Porcupine Mountains. P.J. Hoffmaster sent Gillette on "look-see" visits to areas he was considering for state parks. Upon her return, she would write detailed reports on these areas. She was never paid for this service, although Hoffmeister often was able to pick up her expenses. Sometimes she traveled with her mother, and sometimes she took students from the University of Michigan's Landscape Architecture Department. Often she went alone, because "if Mr. Hoffmaster needed my help and my eyes, I would somehow manage to fit in a trip."[8] She organized the Natural Areas Council to assist in her work, and this organization is still active in studying and recommending properties to the state for protection.

In her own personal career as a landscape architect, she left Breitmeyer and she spent a year as a consultant in Lakeland, Florida, but returned to Michigan to work with the Detroit Parks and Recreation Department as a garden instructor. During the depression she was hired to manage the landscaping for Westacres. Westacres was a low-cost government housing project near Pontiac which included community public gardens. She obtained this job because she was recommended by President Franklin Roosevelt.[9] At the time, she could not believe her good fortune. She subsequently learned that Senator Couzens from Michigan, whom she knew only vaguely, had requested that she supervise this project because he had seen her work with the victory garden project in Detroit and was impressed with what she had accomplished. She worked at Westacres for eight years and eventually opened a private practice in Ann Arbor which she maintained for over 45 years while continuing her conservation efforts. To support herself she created designs for colleges, parks, industries, housing projects, churches, and homes.

In the 1950s, as chair of a conservation committee in the Michigan Botanical Club, she took seriously an assignment to examine the state parks. P.J. Hoffmaster had died suddenly, and the new Director of Conservation was the state geologist and had little interest in parks. Her efforts were noticed, and she received a letter from the Michigan United Conservation Club (MUCC) appointing her to a committee to look into parks. The MUCC was basically a male organization so it was unusual that they asked for her participation.

The committee met monthly on Sunday afternoons at her home to discuss park and recreation problems. The committee members knew that the state had financial troubles and was not interested in parks. They began to look at other states which were popular with tourists and found the same financial troubles and a common pattern of out-of-state visitors. One-third of the park visitors in Michigan were from out-of-state. In the 1950s, this meant five million people were coming every year from somewhere else to visit the state of Michigan. This interstate travel would make a case for federal funds. Gillette realized that the park problems were going to need solutions at both the state and national level, and she resolved to attack the problem politically.

Mr. Wilford Bassett, a legislator from Jackson, was interested in repairing and expanding the state park system, and Gillette read about his efforts. It was his sixth term and everybody respected him, so she asked him how to interest the legislature in the state park problems. Mr. Bassett put her in touch with Dr. William Pierce who was responsible for the

Legislative Research Institute, and Dr. Pierce told her that they definitely needed somebody in the community who was knowledgeable and interested in parks. This advice gave her much encouragement to work for state parks.[10]

Gillette felt she needed facts before she could take action. Budgets for park repairs were unknown at this time, but one day when she was visiting the Department of Conservation, she found a detailed report on what it would take to repair the state parks. An employee said he had put the report together in his spare time and since nobody has asked for it, he hadn't done anything with it.[11] Gillette thought about "this great situation and what on earth to do with it." The year was 1958. She was anxious to "get going" on lobbying for state park repair, but she needed this kind of detail, so she went back to Lansing and asked the employee to leave the room so she could take the report to an office higher up. She carried the report from desk to desk to make sure that everyone in the department knew about it, then she took it into the director's office and told him, "Since you are at the top, you have to decide if the report is accurate." He agreed with the report, and she finally had some facts to work with.

The small committee which met in Ann Arbor on Sundays was ready to organize itself into the Michigan Park Association (MPA). It requested representatives from many organizations, including the Automobile Club, the League of Women Voters, the Federated Garden Clubs of the state of Michigan, the Federated Women's Club, the Park and Forestry Associations, the Michigan Botanical Club, the National Areas Council, labor unions, and every organization which had an interest in parks. Gillette was made president of the MPA and held that position for ten years.[12] The Michigan Park Association encouraged the Department of Natural Resources (formerly the Department of Conservation) to document the financial needs of the state parks and to work on plans for the future. The MPA realized that it needed to work with the state legislature and with the federal government to secure tax money. Lobbying in the legislature was necessary, and Gillette was the only one who had time available. She was 60 years old, however, and had no experience with the legislature. In fact, she had only been in the capital two or three times. Yet she accepted the charge.

A few day later, she received a copy of a shoreline survey from the Department of the Interior. It contained beautiful maps with Great Lakes sites well delineated. She secured a number of shoreline reports and put them in a basket and started off for Lansing, still not knowing if she were doing the right thing. In her own words,

"Every little while on the road it would come over me in a great flood that I was the last person in the world who should attempt any such thing as this. It was just the silliest thing that anybody had ever heard of, for me to go and expect to be able to do anything of consequence over in Lansing. I would turn my car off on a side road and sit there and think about this. Finally the answer came to me that I was the only one to do this and that I had better not sit by the side of the road."[13]

When she arrived at the House of Representatives, she set her basket on the sergeant's desk and said to him,

"I'm Miss Genevieve Gillette, I'm President of the Michigan Parks Association, and I have come to do some work in the legislature. I would like to have you tell me the rules, if you have time now. I don't want to get in trouble here, and I must understand how you do it. I expect the first thing for me to do is to go down to the office where they take care of the lobbyists and straighten things out down there."[14]

The sergeant told her nobody had ever come to talk about parks. She said she knew that and that was why she had come. She was to use the phrase, "I'm Miss Genevieve Gillette, and I have come to tell you about parks," for the next twenty years.

Gillette studied the legislature and the legislators. She began to know the right people to contact about various problems in the parks throughout the state, and she told of her firsthand knowledge about almost every site in the state because she had camped, hiked, or picnicked there. She called on her friends and contacts to talk with state representatives, and she never stopped talking. She also traveled to many representatives' home cities to talk with them in their own environment. She found she could make a big impact this way. She kept notes and soon knew the thinking of almost every representative. They certainly knew of her and her dedication.

The legislature respected her because she knew what she was talking about. She offered to help gather information which they needed and did not try to convince them of particular ideas or ask for money for specific projects. She was representing the Michigan Park Association and had a firm idea of what the organization hoped to accomplish.

Gillette always wore a hat because she found it a good way for the representatives to recognize her. She would introduce herself over the phone by saying, "I'm the lady with the hat," and they would know to whom they were talking. One time she took some feathers off of one of her hats to make fishing lures for a few of the representatives who liked to fish.[15] She loved "having fun that way," and the representatives liked to have her around. She never let them forget that she was

Genevieve Gillette

representing a large organization and encouraged other board members to join her whenever possible.

Soon she asked the legislators for an interim committee to study the state parks. Finally, a committee was established, and two years later it published a revealing report, making the park story much worse than the MPA had ever stated. Gillette was "delighted."[16] The report said investigators saw children in state parks wading in raw sewage because the toilet facilities were not adequate, something she had been hesitant to bring up to the legislature. Five thousand copies of the report were printed and distributed all over the nation. The Michigan legislature was finally aware of the park situation in Michigan and realized it needed to change. Eventually, so much pressure was brought to bear on the governor's office that Governor George Romney requested a one-million-dollar bond issue for parks. The Michigan Parks Association helped to pass the bond issue, insuring financial support for the park system. Gillette and her friends, especially those who were part of the MUCC committee, were delighted. They had predicted it would take them ten years to accomplish the change in attitude towards the parks, and they had been right.

One of Gillette's last and greatest efforts was the work she did to establish Sleeping Bear Dunes as a National Lakeshore. As President of the Michigan Park Association, she was asked to help the National Park Service pass a bill to establish the area as a park. She did not want to work with this project unless the federal government was willing to consider almost twice as much land as was originally earmarked for the park. After analyzing the additional portion of land she suggested, the Park Service was willing to double the acreage, but local residents became angry about the idea of a national park in their area. Gillette spoke in support of the idea at numerous public meetings and stated that the area had been singled out as a unique landscape which should be preserved for the enjoyment of all citizens. When national hearings were scheduled in Washington, D.C., she insisted that the Michigan Park Association Board give testimony. She herself lobbied in congress for three weeks for the Sleeping Bear Dunes Bill and the accompanying Land and Water Bill. Gillette was more convinced than ever that, "the people of the future should not be penalized because their forebearers did not plan to conserve land for the next generation."[17] Both bills passed.

Michigan Senator Philip Hart recognized Gillette as an effective lobbyist and felt she made a difference by coming to Washington to help him. She was later asked by President Lyndon Johnson to serve on the Citizens' Advisory Committee on Natural Beauty. She served on this committee for several years and organized a national conference on scenic roads. Her efforts were appreciated, but she asked to be removed from the committee after four years because she felt she was more effective working in her own state.[18]

In Michigan, she continued to battle the legislature over park and conservation issues even after her eyesight failed. As she aged, it became harder and harder for her to travel to Lansing, but she continued with phone calls and letters. During the last two years of her life her mind began to fail, but she was able to attend her induction into the Michigan Women's Hall of Fame when she received a standing ovation from hundreds of guests. At her death, the Detroit Free Press called her "a saving angel to Michigan's natural beauty" and "a miracle worker." The editorial went on to say:

> For six decades, she haunted lobbyists, legislators and governors with the fervor of an evangel. Her persistence overcame the perennial torpidity of politics, making Michigan a pacesetter among the 50 states for

the conservation and popular enjoyment of its natural resources.[19]

Gillette "took not one penny" for her lifetime of effort as a lobbyist and conservationist. She supported herself in a comfortable way with design work for universities, parks, industries, and private residences. Once, when forced to take an honorarium from the Department of Natural Resources for a talk, she sent back a new picnic table for a park.[20] She was rare, she was selfless, and she took the words "stewardship of the land" to heart.[21] With her down-to-earth language and her plain way of dressing, she was a folk hero to many, but her ability was extraordinary when it came to motivating others and cajoling them into action. She gave direction to the conservation movement in Michigan, saw the state park system grow from one park to over eighty, and lived to see her efforts make a difference.

NOTES

[1] Ablert Fein. "Report on the Profession." <u>Landscape Architecture</u>, October 1972, p. 40.

[2] <u>American Society of Landscape Architects Handbook 1986</u>, p. 27. "Fellows are landscape architects of at least ten years' standing as Members, elected to Fellowship in recognition of their outstanding contributions to the profession by excellence in executed works of landscape architecture, administrative professional work in pubic agencies, professional school instruction, professional writing or direct service to the Society.

[3] Natural Resource Commission, Resolution of tribute to E. Genevieve Gillette, August 12, 1976.

[4] <u>Who's Who in America</u>, 40th edition, p. 1201.

[5] <u>Nature Bulletin No. 608</u>, Forest Preserve District of Cook County, 1960.

[6]Transcripts of E. Genevieve Gillette tapes, 1975, Bentley Historical Library, Tape 16F.

[7]"P.J. Hoffmaster Dies Suddenly", *The Ann Arbor News*, March 25, 1951.

[8]Gillette, Tape 18A.

[9]Gillette, Tape 18B.

[10]Gillette, Tapes 19A and 19B.

[11]Gillette, Tape 20A.

[12]Gillette, Tapes 20A and 20B.

[13]Gillette, Tape 21A.

[14]Gillette, Tape 21A.

[15]Gillette, Tape 21A.

[16]Gillette, Tape 29B.

[17]Gillette, Tapes 23A and 23B.

[18]Christmas letters from Genevieve Gillette to friends, 1965, 1966, and 1969. Genevieve Gillette Nature Center.

[19]"Parks: Miss Gillette was a saving angel to Michigan's natural beauty," *Detroit Free Press*, May 29, 1986.

[20]Ronald Nagel, Director of the State Park Division, Department of Natural Resources, Michigan, personal interview, September 1986.

[21]From the official definition of the profession given by the American Society of Landscape Architectures, Fein, p. 40.

HARRIETTE SIMPSON ARNOW (1908 – 1986)

HARRIETTE SIMPSON ARNOW
NOVELIST

Sharon M. Rambo

The written words of Harriette Simpson Arnow record her vision of forty-five years of American cultural change. Her works chronicle the sweeping changes which characterized our country from the late thirties through the Vietnam War era, and her voice resonates with the storytelling she learned from her maternal grandmother in the southeastern Kentucky hill country where she was born. Her legacy is rich but not large, varied but not predictable. Her published work includes six novels, two social histories, three short stories, one slim autobiography, and five essays. She also left many manuscripts and letters to the University of Kentucky Library.[1] Arnow's works, fiction and nonfiction, tell the lives of those who responded to the romance of explorer Daniel Boone by seeking a new Garden of Eden along the Cumberland River valley in Kentucky. They also tell of a people's growing disillusionment with the realities of modern life--corrupt institutions, rampant technological change, displacement, and bigotry--and their response to these challenges.

Before 1800, Harriette Arnow's ancestors had crossed the mountains from Virginia and the Carolinas. Although not as wealthy as some who migrated west, they were hearty and their faith sustained them. Born July 7, 1908, in Wayne

County, Kentucky, Harriette Lousia Simpson was the daughter of rural schoolteachers, Elias Thomas Simpson and Mollie Jane Denney Simpson. They soon moved to Burnside, a lumbering town 90 miles south of Lexington on the Cumberland River, because her father needed the larger income of bookkeeper to accommodate his growing family.[2] Elias and Mollie Jane Simpson raised six children on nearly forty acres, high on a hill above Burnside, and their lives were similar to the vast number of others who settled on the land in the early twentieth century. Arnow's childhood activities were those common to most girls—making candy, baking cakes, sewing, riding the mules, walking in the woods, playing games, and visiting the river.

From an early age, Harriette Simpson Arnow knew the importance of telling life's stories. She came from a family of storytellers and singers and consequently gained knowledge of her ancestors and their struggles through these family entertainments. In an interview recorded by William Eckley, Arnow remembers a childhood of expanding upon the memories of others to formulate a narrative:

> Sometimes I changed them to my liking; foggy times were good for this; and we had in fall and winter many such gray days when the sky was lower than our hill. Wraiths of fog wandered about all day long, and even when the rain stopped, the woods dripped still as from a heavy dew; and all sounds came clearly up from the hidden world below us like sound heard through water...It was in the gray stillness with the smell of cedar, of wet earth, and the fainter smell of decaying limestone all about me, that I remade the memories as I wanted them to be. True there was confusion; the past, present, and the stories I was beginning to read were all mingled in my head.[3]

During much of her childhood, Arnow listened to these retellings of the past--personal histories full of witchcraft, war, and life in the hills. Her family also spent what little it could afford on books to supplement the children's education. Birthday and Christmas celebrations frequently meant the gift of a book; and the books she received for her sixth Christmas included Swiss Family Robinson, and Robinson Crusoe, soon followed by Pilgrim's Progress and the works by Charles Dickens. At ten she received Idylls of the King, and "The Rime of the Ancient Mariner." More traditional educational books were also included--stories of the Bible, myths of Greece and Rome, the lives of musicians and artists, and volumes of local history. Arnow admitted a preference for fiction because it permitted her "to change it in my head afterwards."[4]

Her early formal education was a blend of reading, arithmetic, spelling, art, and games. In fourth grade, her story was chosen to be read to the class, a story about the thing she had always wanted--a big writing desk full of cubby holes and drawers. In the same year, her Grandmother Denny died. She had been the matriarch and famed storyteller, and the loss greatly touched the Simpson family. Their financial situation necessitated the father's relocating to a remote county as a tool dresser in the oil fields. Soon, Mollie Jane Simpson and the children joined him, fleeing loneliness and the Asian flu epidemic. As there was no school, she taught the children at home. In 1919 Arnow and her sister attended a boarding school in St. Helens, Kentucky. Arnow was ready for high school by twelve and transferred to Stanton Academy, not far from her family's home. Again, she excelled, especially in writing. At a teacher's request she read one of her stories to the Academy Literary Club.[5] Financial difficulties caused the family to return to Burnside and, even though Arnow was offered a work scholarship to continue at Stanton, her parents chose to have her attend high school in Burnside so she could help her ailing mother with household duties.

Her high school years showed other accommodation to change. Because she had been advanced two years, her current Burnside classmates were none of her former friends. In addition, her mother's new baby meant increased household duties. The curriculum of Burnside High School compared poorly to Stanton Academy, although Arnow enjoyed an agriculture class and a three-year history sequence.[6] Literary and Debating Clubs challenged her skills, but her parents' attitude toward her desire to write frustrated her. They considered writing a waste of time and energy, but she persevered, submitting a fairy tale about the flowers in a nearby valley to Child Life. The story was not accepted; however, she continued to work on her writing throughout high school.

Although women received the vote in 1920, and some other barriers to woman's equality were being erased, Arnow's future was to be traditional. Her parents wanted their daughters to be teachers: to attend college for two years and be prepared to teach at eighteen, thereby earning a living until marriage. So she entered Berea College, a choice which offered new and unexpected challenges. The requirement of a fundamentalist Christian lifestyle--in labor, dress, and social regulations--weighed heavily on a spirit attuned to more freedom. Her "labor included washing dishes and working two hours a day in a tourist shop, weaving thread into cloth for towels, tablecloths and other items. The dress code meant no silk stocking, not rolling the stockings, no bare skin except the arm and a little neck; one was never to be 'suggestive'."[7] The academic life pleased her, however, and she liked her classes in geology, botany, and English literature. She could have continued on a botany scholarship after her second year, but her older sister's desire to quit teaching and return to school meant that Arnow, not yet eighteen, had to leave college and begin teaching.

Her first school, in a fairly remote part of Kentucky, reflected the poverty in the community. Fourteen undernourished and isolated students came to a meagerly furnished one-room building. But Arnow experienced much among these hospitable and struggling backwoods people and her first novel, Mountain Path, incorporates material from these times. She continued reading voluminously and studying the short story in a correspondence course from the University of Kentucky.

After another year as teacher and principal in a two-year elementary school, Arnow moved to Louisville, resolved to finish her bachelor's degree. During this time, she matured significantly. She borrowed money, lived in the YWCA, worked odd jobs to support herself, and enjoyed the cultural live of the city. She graduated in 1930, the same year her father died. While in Louisville, she continued to refine her writing and joined Chi Delta Phi, a literary-writing society, but finances forced a return to teaching in rural Pulaski County. Although this community was more prosperous and worldly than that of her first assignment, she still preferred the city and so, after a year and a half, she accepted a junior high teaching position in Louisville. Soon the rigors of teaching social science to six groups of different abilities overwhelmed her and she was hospitalized. Upon recovering, she spent the summer as a waitress at a Michigan resort, the Country Inn of Petosky, where she had worked during college; there she resolved to do no more teaching. The financial demands of her siblings eased as they left home and Arnow began what was to become her first novel, Mountain Path.[8]

Seeking challenge and opportunity, she moved to Cincinnati, where she worked as a waitress, expanded herself by reading Russian, English, and French literature, and wrote whenever she could. She published several short stories and continued the character sketches begun while in northern Michigan. She then sent the series of sketches to Macmillan Publishing Company which rejected them but enclosed an encouraging letter. At the same time, and in response to a story published elsewhere, Harold Strauss, an editor for a major publisher, sought out the young author. He judged the character sketches, now called Path, to be of "no regular class but to have such extraordinary quality of their own as to be completely self-justifying."[9] Strauss encouraged her to convert the sketches into a dramatic novel with a major narrative line for continuity and Arnow followed his advice. She quit her jobs as waitress and typist and "laid in a great deal of condensed milk and oatmeal and bread and did nothing but write until I had what I thought was a novel."[10] In 1936, when Arnow was twenty eight, her first novel, Mountain Path, was published by Covici Friede.

Mountain Path was well received by reviewers. The book seems autobiographical for she certainly drew on her own experiences for the adventures of Louisa Sheridan, a school teacher in the remote Kentucky hills; however, the story is not about Arnow. The careful characterization and setting in Mountain Path rise above the melodramatic feuding, moonshining, and romance of the plot. Her family did not approve of the book and would have preferred "nicer" people as characters and publicity which avoided referring to their daughter as a waitress. They were also concerned that readers would assume she herself "had fallen in love with a moonshiner."[11] She continued to study other writers, especially the Realists whom Harold Strauss recommended and soon began another novel, the unpublished Between the

Flowers. Somewhat adrift after the rejection of this novel and finding the Realism of those such as James Farrell and Vardis Fisher "not necessarily true," she began to write for the Federal Writers Project, all the time becoming more socially and historically knowledgeable about the Cumberland.[12]

Her 1939 marriage to Harold Arnow, a writer and newspaper man, continued the pattern of challenge and struggle. He had material for a book about his recent three-year sojourn in Alaska, and she had writing of her own. Together, they settled on a place they named "Submarginal Manor." It was beautiful land purchased at a very low price, with an old log house needing much repair, water carried from a spring, and heat supplied by coal dug from around the premises. In December 1939, their first child was stillborn, and soon after her recovery, Arnow began teaching again, this time in a one-room school. And again, her writing became secondary. She remembers, "We were so busy subsisting there was not time to write."[13] It was at this time, however, that she began a novel which was published ten years later as Hunter's Horn. She also had several articles published in Atlantic Monthly and Writer's Digest.

The birth of a daughter, Marcella, in 1941, caused the Arnows to seek a less remote abode. Early in 1944, Harold moved to Detroit as a reporter for the Detroit Times, and Harriette followed after selling the various livestock. In the temporary wartime housing project in which they lived, Arnow finished Hunter's Horn and absorbed the rich background which was to come to life in The Dollmaker. Here were people vastly different from any she had ever known--people from all religious and economic backgrounds and from various sections of the country, all coming together in wartime Detroit. The family expanded in December 1946 with the birth of a son, Thomas. Like most women writers, Arnow found that writing and housewifery meant compromise, and she began getting up at four o'clock in the morning to write before her family arose. In 1949 Hunter's Horn was published. It tells of Nunn Ballew, a man whose obsession with catching a red fox leads him to neglect his family and his land. It received a best-novel-of-the-year award in a national critic's poll, winning over Orwell's 1984, and was translated into several foreign languages. Soon after, the Arnows moved out of the city and built a house near Ann Arbor. In spite of the relative freedom provided by such a rural setting, Harriette admitted that "...it meant a second car and I drove the children back and forth to school just as I suppose hundred of thousands of other mothers so situated do. It didn't leave much time for writing. My problems, I suppose, are like the problems of a great many other women who hope to carry on after marriage and discover they cannot do as they did before."[14]

She continued to write, however, working in a den furnished with chairs and desks built specifically to accommodate her small stature.[15] The Dollmaker, published in 1954, was voted best novel of the year in Saturday Review's national critics' poll and finished second to William Faulkner's The Fable for the National Book Award. Three nonfiction, social history books followed: Seed Time on the Cumberland, Flowering of the Cumberland, and Old Burnside; also, two novels, The Weedkiller's Daughter and The Kentucky Trace. Until her death in 1986, one year after her husband's, she continued to write and rewrite.

Of special interest to residents of Michigan are her two novels with this state as setting. Separated in publication by sixteen years, both The Dollmaker and The Weedkiller's Daughter detail the efforts of individuals to reconcile memories with reality in order to survive. Struggle and isolation characterize much of the lives of Gertie Nevels and

Susan Schnitzer, heroes respectively of the two Michigan novels.

Gertie's self described "whittlin' foolishness" unifies the The Dollmaker. The carved wooden dolls and crucifixes are her efforts to reconcile memories of Kentucky life as a subsistence farmer with a Detroit reality of few possibilities. The first third of the book details that early 1940's Kentucky life of occasional schooling and mail delivery: no running water, electricity, plumbing, or doctors. Gertie dreams to someday be free of the landlord and on a farm of her own; instead, she succumbs to her female duty to follow her husband, Clovis, to Detroit when he responds to his male, patriotic duty to be a wartime factory worker. And just as Gertie wields her knife to create figures from wood, she, too, is carved and sculpted by her life in Merry Hill, a wartime housing development.

The causes of Gertie's physical and emotional alienation are several: a war which causes dislocation; socio-economic conflict, with "ole man Flint" and his factories against the labor movement; self erasure by abandoning old ways and learning new ones; a language of unknown and foreign words--communists, Jew, nigger, overtime, Red Squad; and, most abhorent to Gertie, buying necessities on credit. Gertie sees physical surroundings that are "as if somewhere far away a piece of hell had come up from underground,...a gray wasteland" (168-169). Life in Merry Hill means tragedy: for Gertie, the loss of two of her five children; for her neighbors, unceasing accomodation. Together they experience alienation and isolation but also personal validation.

Susan Schnitzer of The Weedkiller's Daughter struggles to reconcile her memories of a better life with the reality of a late 1960's elite Detroit suburb--computers, would-be high school psychologists, post-McCarthy paranoia, familial alienation, and environmental devastation. Being a teenage in

Eden Hills means being out of focus, somewhere between a forbidden past—early years with an adoring maternal grandmother and the joys of nature in Nova Scotia—and an unacceptable, alienating present inhabited by a father whom she calls Bismark and a mother, the Popsicle Queen. Susie's life is a conflict between appearances and reality. She appears a dutiful daughter but, in truth, she is an exile, thoroughly contemptuous of her father and his efforts to eradicate weeds, that is, to rid his world of all those who violate his version of the American Dream—Negroes, Jews, Communists, hillbillies. A monument to the artificial, Susie's mother represents the millions of women whose personal identity is crushed into an unthinking uniformity.

Surrounded by the annihilating and synthetic, Susie's challenge is to avoid discovery as an imposter while forging her own true self. Her neighborhood schoolmates have also been scarred by the times, be it the hypocrisy at school, the American war against the Vietnamese, or the destruction of the nearby farmlands to build an exclusive subdivision. Joining with the youthful misfits is The Primitive. The Primitive is Gertie Nevels of the first novel, owner of a large tract of land, a hermit who personally takes up arms to block neighborhood despoilation. Susie's love of nature transcends The Primitive's singleness of purpose and specifies itself in a love of the sea, a love rooted in memories and symbolic of the freedom she craves. When Susie and a male friend prevent a sailing accident on Lake Erie, she discovers within herself the confidence necessary to challege the restrictions of Eden Hills society.

Both of Arnow's Michigan novels exhibit the richness of detail typical of her storytelling. The struggle of Gertie in The Dollmaker mirrors that of her Merry Hill neighbors, particularly the women. Gertie survives the loss of children and the sacrifice of leaving Kentucky. Susie, the hero of The

Weedkiller's Daughter, survives the conditioning of her family and society, but her future is a vision dark with the bequests of war and the poisoning of the environment. Both novels show that the memories of an innocent past are essential to surviving the cruel encroachments of modern life. Arnow's characters, like herself, are strong and sensitive, and although they bend, they do not break.

NOTES

[1] Major Works of Harriette Arnow include five novels: Mountain Path, (1936); Hunter's Horn, (1949); The Dollmaker, (1954); The Weedkiller's Daughter, (1970); The Kentucky Trace: A Novel of the American Revolution, (1974); one autobiography: Old Burnside, (1977); and Social Histories: Seedtime on the Cumberland, (1960) and Flowering of the Cumberland, (1963).

[2] Eckley, William. Harriette Arnow. New York: Twayne's United States Authors Series (#245), 1974, p. 18.

[3] Quoted in Eckley, p. 22.

[4] Quoted in Eckley, p. 24.

[5] Eckley, p. 28.

[6] Eckley, p. 30.

[7] Quoted in Eckley, p. 32.

[8] Eckley, p. 37.

[9] Eckley, p. 39.

[10] Kotlowitz, Alex. "At 75, Full Speed Ahead." Detroit News Magazine, 4 Dec 1983, p. 22.

[11] Eckley, p. 39.

[12] Eckley, p. 40.

[13] Kotlowitz, p. 22.

[14] Quoted in Eckley, p. 43.

[15] Kotlowitz, p. 26.